Series / Number 07-118

INTERACTION EFFECTS
IN FACTORIAL ANALYSIS
OF VARIANCE

JAMES JACCARD
University at Albany, State University of New York

SAGE PUBLICATIONS
The International Professional Publishers
Thousand Oaks   London   New Delhi

For information:

SAGE Publications, Inc.
2455 Teller Road
Thousand Oaks, California 91320
E-mail: order@sagepub.com

SAGE Publications Ltd.
6 Bonhill Street
London EC2A 4PU
United Kingdom

SAGE Publications India Pvt. Ltd.
M-32 Market
Greater Kailash I
New Delhi 110 048 India

Printed in the United States of America

Library of Congress Cataloging-in-Publication Data

Jaccard, James.
    Interaction effects in factorial analysis of variance / by James Jaccard.
      p. cm.—(Sage university papers series. Quantitative applications in the
social sciences ; no. 07-118)
    Includes bibliographical references (p.). ISBN 0-7619-1221-5
  (pbk. : acid-free paper) 1. Social sciences—Statistical methods. 2. Analysis of variance.
  3. Factor analysis. I. Title. II. Series.
    HA29.J227 1998
    519.5′354—dc21   97-33807

98 99 00 01 02 03 04 10 9 8 7 6 5 4 3 2 1

Acquiring Editor:	C. Deborah Laughton
Editorial Assistant:	Eileen Carr
Production Editor:	Michele Lingre
Production Assistant:	Lynn Miyata
Typesetter/Designer:	Yang-hee Syn Maresca
Print Buyer:	Anna Chin

When citing a university paper, please use the proper form. Remember to cite the Sage University Paper series title and include the paper number. One of the following formats can be adapted (depending on the style manual used):

(1) Jaccard, J. (1998) *Interaction Effects in Factorial Analysis of Variance.* Sage University Papers Series on Quantitative Applications in the Social Sciences, 07-118. Thousand Oaks, CA: Sage.

OR

(2) Jaccard, J. (1998). *Interaction effects in factorial analysis of variance* (Sage University Papers Series on Quantitative Applications in the Social Sciences, series no. 07-118). Thousand Oaks, CA: Sage.

CONTENTS

SERIES EDITOR'S INTRODUCTION

Analysis of variance (ANOVA), the central analytic technique for experimenters, was the topic of the very first monograph in our series (Iversen & Norpoth, *Analysis of Variance*, No. 1). Subsequently, we have covered different aspects of ANOVA (Spector, *Research Designs*, No. 23; Bray & Maxwell, *Multivariate Analysis of Variance*, No. 54; Klockars & Sax, *Multiple Comparisons*, No. 61; Brown & Melamed, *Experimental Design and Analysis*, No. 74; Girden, *ANOVA: Repeated Measures*, No. 84; Toothaker, *Multiple Comparison Procedures*, No. 89; Jackson & Brashers, *Random Factors in ANOVA*, No. 98). However, none of these efforts featured the critical subject of interaction effects. Professor Jaccard is, arguably, the world's leading expert on interaction effects, having taken the lead in two previous volumes (*Interaction Effects in Multiple Regression*, No. 72; *LISREL Approaches to Interaction Effects in Multiple Regression*, No. 114). In this current monograph, he deftly extends himself to ANOVA users.

What is an interaction effect? Following a classic definition, it would exist when the effect of one independent variable (X_1) on a dependent variable (Y) depends on the value of another independent variable (X_2). Suppose that a political scientist wants to conduct an experiment to assess the impact of gender on political contributions. The subjects (100 registered voters) are exposed to a 15-minute campaign speech, the same across groups except for the gender of the candidate. It is a 2×2 factorial design, where X_1 = gender of the candidate, X_2 = gender of the voter, and Y = total dollars out of a \$100 that the voter wishes to contribute after hearing the speech. The interaction hypothesis is that the effect of the *focal* independent variable, X_1, depends on the *moderator* variable, X_2. In other words, voter gender changes the impact of candidate gender on contributions. To test this hypothesis, one could evaluate the difference between two mean differences from the following table:

	Gender of Voter	
	Male	Female
Gender of candidate		
Male	80	70
Female	40	60

One can see that male candidates are more likely to get contributions, especially if the voter is male. Calculating the value of the difference between the mean differences, to assess the interaction effect, yields $(80 - 40) - (70 - 60) = (40) - (10) = 30$. Applying a significance test, we could determine whether this nonzero value is large enough to reject the null.

This approach sees interaction effects as the differences between mean differences. An alternative sees interaction effects in terms of residualized means, where cell means are adjusted for main effects. Most researchers follow the former approach, and Jaccard favors it. However, he is careful to say it is not a matter of "right" or "wrong" but rather a question of selecting one statistical procedure over another, recognizing that the different results can lead to different conclusions. A helpful regression analogy is offered. The first approach parallels dummy variable regression with the usual (0, 1) coding of the independent variables. In the forgoing example, X_1 and X_2 would be scored 0 or 1 and regressed, along with product term $X_1 \times X_2$, on Y. The second approach runs the same dummy variable regression except with effects coding $(+1, -1)$ for the independent variables.

Jaccard does an excellent job of presenting other controversies in factorial ANOVA and the analysis of interaction effects. He thoroughly explicates two important alternatives to classical hypothesis testing: magnitude estimation (effect size) and interval estimation (confidence intervals). Treatment is evenhanded and gives readers the ability to employ these alternatives if they so desire. This ability is enhanced by devoting an entire chapter to working through the well-chosen example of the role of peers in getting information on drunk driving to high school students.

More complex design issues are considered in the latter chapters. A 3×2 factorial design is unfolded with steps provided for analyzing interaction effects with degrees of freedom greater than 1. Step-by-step procedures also are conveniently offered for dissecting higher order interactions. The final chapter focuses on assumptions with special attention given to the problems of unequal sample size and measurement error. Jaccard makes a strong case for application of the interval-level assumption when the approximation is good. Finally, he issues an important warning: The various statistical packages used to carry out the interaction analysis—STATISTICA, SPSS, SAS—may report different parameter estimates. Care must be taken to read the fine print on the options and output of the particular program selected. Jaccard's attention to detail, combined with clear guidelines to the practicing researcher, characterizes this highly successful text.

—*Michael S. Lewis-Beck*
Series Editor

INTERACTION EFFECTS IN FACTORIAL ANALYSIS OF VARIANCE

JAMES JACCARD
University of Albany, State University of New York

PREFACE

Factorial analysis of variance is widely used in the social sciences. A powerful feature of factorial designs is their ability to evaluate interaction effects. Despite its ubiquity, the meaning and testing of interaction effects in factorial designs remains a matter of some confusion. The recent exchanges among Rosnow, Rosenthal, and others indicate this state of affairs (e.g., Meyer, 1991; Rosnow & Rosenthal, 1989a, 1991, 1996; Petty, Fabrigar, Wegener, & Priester, 1996). In addition, there are widespread differences in procedures that researchers use to decompose and explicate interaction effects, especially for interactions with more than a single degree of freedom. One purpose of this monograph is to describe, on a conceptual level, general issues underlying the analysis of interaction effects in factorial designs.

Classic hypothesis testing has come increasingly under attack, and many methodologists suggest alternative methods of analysis that can either supplement or replace the classic approach. Among the popular alternatives are magnitude estimation, interval estimation, and Bayesian approaches. I also introduce readers to methods for analysis of interactions using the former two approaches. I omit the Bayesian perspective because of its complexity in practice and because I believe it is best treated in the context of a more detailed textbook focused on Bayesian principles and applications.

I assume that readers already are familiar with the fundamentals of analysis of variance. My presentation, however, is introductory and nontechnical and is intended to reach applied researchers rather than those specializing in the study of statistics and methodology.

I would like to thank several of my colleagues for their feedback on earlier drafts, including Hart Blanton, David Brinberg, Michael Lewis-Beck, Glenn Sanders, Robert McDonald, and two anonymous reviewers. Their input was extremely useful, and I am grateful for their efforts.

1. INTRODUCTION

Factorial analysis of variance (ANOVA) is widely used in the social sciences. It is commonly recognized that one of the advantages of a factorial design is that it permits the researcher to analyze interaction effects between independent variables relative to the dependent variable. Despite the ubiquity of factorial designs, the analysis of interaction effects often proves to be confusing. Even a cursory examination of the research literature reveals that the statistical practices used by social scientists for analyzing interaction effects are not uniform across studies that employ comparable designs. For example, some analysts use different error terms when following up a statistically significant interaction effect. Some analysts pursue simple main-effects analysis after a statistically significant interaction effect, whereas others focus on interaction comparisons or orthogonal interaction contrasts. Some analysts control for experimentwise error rates, whereas others do not. Indeed, there is even controversy about exactly what constitutes an interaction effect in factorial ANOVA (e.g., Meyer, 1991; Rosnow & Rosenthal, 1989a, 1989b, 1991, 1996).

This monograph is designed to elucidate the nature of interaction effects in factorial designs and to clarify issues in their analysis. In this chapter, we first consider different ways of characterizing interactions in the context of a fixed-effects factorial ANOVA.[1] We describe the traditional hypothesis-testing approach to interaction analysis and characterize the statistical assumptions underlying this framework. In Chapter 2, we consider alternative approaches to analyzing interaction effects that focus on effect size methodology and interval estimation rather than on traditional hypothesis testing. We summarize criticisms of classic null hypothesis testing and present practical guidelines for pursuing the magnitude estimation and interval estimation approaches. Chapter 3 presents a complete numerical example applying the concepts of Chapters 1 and 2. In Chapter 4, we consider more complex designs, namely designs that involve more than two levels and designs with three or more factors. Finally, Chapter 5 focuses on selected issues related to interaction analysis including what to do when statistical assumptions are violated, the biasing effects of measurement error, the case of unequal cell sample sizes, and computer applications.

TABLE 1.1

Means and Summary Table for Sentence Severity Example

| | Ethnicity of Juror | | |
Ethnicity of Perpetrator	Caucasian	African American	Row Mean
Caucasian	10.00	14.00	12.00
African American	18.00	12.00	15.00
Column mean	14.00	13.00	
Grand mean = 13.50			

Source	SS	df	MS	F	p
Ethnicity of perpetrator (A)	180.00	1	180.00	11.31	< .001
Ethnicity of juror (B)	20.00	1	20.00	1.26	< .266
A × B	500.00	1	500.00	31.40	< .001
Within	1,210.00	76	15.92		
Total	1,910.00	79			

NOTE: SS = sum of squares; MS = mean square.

1.1 Conceptualizations of Interaction Effects

The concept of interaction is best developed in the context of a 2×2 factorial design. Consider the following example. A researcher was interested in whether the ethnicity of a person found to be guilty of a crime might influence how severe a juror feels that the punishment should be for the crime. A total of 80 individuals were presented with a vignette describing the occurrence of a brutal rape and a characterization of the ensuing trial. After reading the scenario, the individuals were asked to indicate the number of years that the perpetrator should serve in prison as punishment for the crime. The vignettes were identical for all research participants with one exception: Half of the individuals were told that the perpetrator was Caucasian, whereas the other half were told that the perpetrator was African American. The second factor in this study was the ethnicity of the research participant (i.e., the juror), and it was defined such that half of the research participants were Caucasian and the other half were African American. This yielded a 2×2 fixed-effects, between-subjects factorial design consisting of the ethnicity of the perpetrator and the ethnicity of the juror, with a sample size of 20 per cell. Table 1.1 presents the relevant mean values and the ANOVA summary table. It can be seen that there was a significant

($p < .05$) main effect of the ethnicity of the perpetrator and a significant ($p < .05$) interaction effect.

1.1.1 Interaction Effects as the Difference Between Mean Differences

A common approach to the analysis of interactions is to conceptualize an interaction effect as the difference between mean differences. This subsection explicates the logic of this conceptual orientation.

In the aforementioned example, there are three sets of null and alternative hypotheses that traditionally are examined. The first set focuses on the main effect of the ethnicity of the perpetrator and can be stated as follows:

$$H_0: \mu_{CP} - \mu_{AP} = 0$$
$$H_1: \mu_{CP} - \mu_{AP} \neq 0$$

where μ_{CP} is the population mean on the dependent variable for the Caucasian perpetrator (collapsing across ethnicity of the juror) and μ_{AP} is the population mean on the dependent variable for the African American perpetrator (collapsing across ethnicity of the juror).

The second set of hypotheses focuses on the main effect of the ethnicity of the juror and is stated as follows:

$$H_0: \mu_{CJ} - \mu_{AJ} = 0$$
$$H_1: \mu_{CJ} - \mu_{AJ} \neq 0$$

where μ_{CJ} is the population mean on the dependent variable for the case of the Caucasian juror (collapsing across ethnicity of the perpetrator) and μ_{AJ} is the population mean on the dependent variable for the African American juror (collapsing across ethnicity of the perpetrator).

The third set of hypotheses focuses on the interaction effect. An interaction effect can be said to exist when the effect of an independent variable on a dependent variable differs depending on the value of a third variable, commonly called a moderator variable. This *moderator approach* to interaction analysis requires that the theorist specify a moderator variable and what is called a *focal* independent variable, namely the independent variable whose effect on the dependent variable is said to be moderated by the moderator variable. To specify null and alternative hypotheses for the interaction effect, the researcher first chooses one of the factors to be the moderator variable. In the present case, we use the ethnicity of the juror as the moderator variable. An interaction effect is said to exist if the effect of ethnicity of the perpetrator on the judged severity of the punishment differs as a function of the ethnicity of the juror. This can be stated formally in terms of null and alternative hypotheses as follows:

$$H_0: (\mu_{CP,CJ} - \mu_{AP,CJ}) - (\mu_{CP,AJ} - \mu_{AP,AJ}) = 0$$
$$H_1: (\mu_{CP,CJ} - \mu_{AP,CJ}) - (\mu_{CP,AJ} - \mu_{AP,AJ}) \neq 0$$

where $\mu_{CP,CJ}$ is the population mean for the case of the Caucasian perpetrator as rated by Caucasian jurors, $\mu_{AP,CJ}$ is the population mean for the case of the African American perpetrator as rated by Caucasian jurors, $\mu_{CP,AJ}$ is the population mean for the case of the Caucasian perpetrator as rated by African American jurors, and $\mu_{AP,AJ}$ is the population mean for the case of the African American perpetrator as rated by African American jurors. Examine the null hypothesis (H_0). The first term in parentheses ($\mu_{CP,CJ} - \mu_{AP,CJ}$) reflects the effect of varying the ethnicity of the perpetrator, but only for Caucasian jurors. The second term in parentheses ($\mu_{CP,AJ} - \mu_{AP,AJ}$) also reflects the effect of varying the ethnicity of the perpetrator, but only for African American jurors. If these two effects are the same, then the difference between them will be zero and there is no interaction effect; the effect of the independent variable (ethnicity of the perpetrator) on the dependent variable (judged severity of punishment) is the same at each level of the moderator variable (ethnicity of the juror). This is the essence of moderator conceptions of interaction effects.

From a statistical standpoint, the designation of one of the independent variables as a moderator variable is arbitrary. If we select the ethnicity of the juror to be the moderator variable, then the null hypothesis for the interaction effect is

$$H_0: (\mu_{CP,CJ} - \mu_{AP,CJ}) - (\mu_{CP,AJ} - \mu_{AP,AJ}) = 0$$

If, instead, we select the ethnicity of the perpetrator as the moderator variable, then the null hypothesis is

$$H_0: (\mu_{CP,AJ} - \mu_{CP,CJ}) - (\mu_{AP,AJ} - \mu_{AP,CJ}) = 0$$

These two expressions are algebraically equivalent (i.e., if one is true, then the other must be true), so the choice of a moderator variable is determined completely by theoretical or conceptual considerations. It is our experience that most formal research questions naturally lend themselves to the specification of one of the variables as having *moderator* status and that such a designation is a useful heuristic for thinking about interactions.

The designation of a moderator variable on conceptual grounds often is straightforward. For example, suppose one wants to determine whether the effectiveness of a clinical treatment for depression is more or less effective for males than for females. It is evident in this case that gender is the moderator variable and that the presence or absence of the treatment is the focal independent variable. On the other hand, there are situations in which one theorist's moderator variable might be another theorist's focal independent variable and vice versa (Abelson, 1995). For example, a consumer psychologist who studies product quality and choice might be interested in the effect of product quality on brand preference and how this is moderated by pricing structure. By contrast, a marketing researcher using the same experimental paradigms as the consumer psychologist might be interested in the effect of pricing structure on brand preference and how this is moderated by product quality. In each case, the designation of the moderator variable follows directly from the theoretical orientation of the researcher. Neither specification is better than the other, and the results of the interaction analysis will be statistically identical. The two designations simply represent different perspectives on the same phenomenon.

The preceding formulation illustrates one way in which interaction effects have been conceptualized in a 2×2 factorial design, namely as the difference between two mean differences. Each mean difference reflects the effects of an independent variable on a dependent variable at a given level of another variable (i.e., the moderator variable), and the central question is whether these differences (i.e., effects) differ as a function of the levels of the moderator variable.

For the data in Table 1.1, the sample values for the main effect of ethnicity of the perpetrator were $\overline{X}_{CP} - \overline{X}_{AP} = 12.00 - 15.00 = -3.00$. Although the difference between sample means is nonzero and appears to be consistent with the alternative hypothesis for this main effect, the traditional question of interest is whether the sample difference in means (-3.00) could reasonably be attributed to sampling error given a true null hypothesis. The F test in Table 1.1 suggests that this is unlikely (because the probability of obtaining the observed sample mean difference or a difference that is more extreme, assuming the null hypothesis is true, is less than the traditional alpha level of .05).

The sample mean values for the main effect of ethnicity of the juror were $\overline{X}_{CJ} - \overline{X}_{AJ} = 14.00 - 13.00 = 1.00$. This value also is nonzero and appears to be consistent with the alternative hypothesis for the main effect. However, the F test in Table 1.1 indicates that a sampling error interpretation under the assumption of a true null hypothesis cannot be ruled out with confidence.

The sample values for the interaction effect were $(\overline{X}_{CP,CJ} - \overline{X}_{AP,CJ}) - (\overline{X}_{CP,AJ} - \overline{X}_{AP,AJ}) = (10.00 - 18.00) - (14.00 - 12.00) = -8.00 - 2.00 = -10.00$. The value of the difference between the mean differences is nonzero, and, as seen in Table 1.1, the traditional null hypothesis is rejected (because $p < .05$).

1.1.2 Interaction Effects as Treatment Effects

Several methodologists have objected to the characterization of interaction effects as differences between mean differences (e.g., Rosnow & Rosenthal, 1989a, 1989b, 1991). These analysts conceptualize interaction effects in terms of *treatment effects* or in terms of the analysis of *residualized means* as developed in the context of the classic ANOVA model. Consider first the main effect of ethnicity of the perpetrator. What is the effect, if any, of the perpetrator being African American? The grand mean collapsing across all factors in the study represents the average severity rating for all individuals. We designate this parameter as μ_G. The effect of the perpetrator being African American can be defined as

$$\tau_{AP} = \mu_{AP} - \mu_G$$

where τ_{AP} is the treatment effect for the case of the African American perpetrator and all other terms are as defined previously. For the sample data in Table 1.1, the grand mean ($\overline{X}_G$) was 13.50. This means that, on average, individuals in the study said that the perpetrator should serve 13.50 years in prison. The mean for African American perpetrators was 15.00, which is 1.50 years higher than the grand mean. Thus, the sample estimate of the population treatment effect is

$$t_{AP} = \overline{X}_{AP} - \overline{X}_G = 15.00 - 13.50 = 1.50$$

The effect of being an African American perpetrator is, on average, to raise the judged level of punishment by 1.50 years above the typical severity rating (i.e., the grand mean). Although this sample treatment effect is nonzero, the traditional question of interest is whether the observed treatment effect could reasonably be attributed to sampling error, assuming that the population treatment effect is zero. Stated another way, the null hypothesis is that the population treatment effect for the African American perpetrator is zero, and the alternative hypothesis is that the population treatment effect for the African American perpetrator is not zero. Of interest is the probability (p value) of observing the nonzero sample treatment effect (or a treatment effect that is more extreme) under the assumption that the null hypothesis is true. If this p value is low (e.g., $p < .05$), then the null hypothesis of a zero population treatment effect is rejected.

Let us now examine the treatment effect for the second level of the ethnicity of the perpetrator factor. Using similar logic, this is defined as

$$\tau_{CP} = \mu_{CP} - \mu_G$$

where τ_{CP} is the treatment effect for the case of the Caucasian perpetrator. For the sample data in Table 1.1, the estimate of this population treatment effect is

$$t_{CP} = \overline{X}_{CP} - \overline{X}_G = 12.00 - 13.50 = -1.50$$

The effect of being a Caucasian perpetrator is, on average, to lower the level of punishment 1.50 years below the typical severity rating, as indicated by the grand mean.

Note that these treatment effects for the two levels of ethnicity of the perpetrator are equal in value but opposite in sign. This is a mathematical truism that always will hold for the case of a factor with only two levels. It also is the case that the sum of the treatment effects across the levels of a factor always will equal zero, and this is true even for factors with more than two levels.

Traditionally, if an F ratio associated with a factor in an ANOVA is statistically significant, then this means that at least one of the sample treatment effects defined by the levels of the factor is statistically significant (i.e., the null hypothesis of a zero population treatment effect for at least one of the treatment effects is rejected). In the case where there are only two levels of a factor, a statistically significant F ratio implies that both of the treatment effects are statistically significant (because with two levels, the effects are of equal magnitude but opposite in sign). Thus, for the data in Table 1.1, both treatment effects for the ethnicity of the perpetrator factor are statistically significant.

A similar analysis can be conducted for the main effect of the ethnicity of the juror. The treatment effect for African American jurors is defined as

$$\tau_{AJ} = \mu_{AJ} - \mu_G$$

where τ_{AJ} is the treatment effect for the case of the African American juror. For the sample data in Table 1.1, the mean for African American jurors was 13.00, which is 0.50 years lower than the grand mean. Thus, the sample estimate of the population treatment effect is

$$t_{AJ} = \overline{X}_{AJ} - \overline{X}_G = 13.00 - 13.50 = -0.50$$

The effect of being an African American juror is, on average, to lower the level of punishment by 0.50 years below the typical severity rating, as indicated by the grand mean. The treatment effect for the second level of the ethnicity of the juror factor is

$$\tau_{CJ} = \mu_{CJ} - \mu_G,$$

where τ_{CJ} is the treatment effect for the case of the Caucasian juror. For the sample data in Table 1.1, the sample estimate of this population treatment effect is

$$t_{CJ} = \overline{X}_{CJ} - \overline{X}_G = 14.00 - 13.50 = 0.50$$

The effect of being a Caucasian juror is, on average, to raise the level of punishment 0.50 years above the typical severity rating, as indicated by the grand mean. As seen in the summary table of Table 1.1, the null hypothesis of nonzero treatment effects for this factor cannot be rejected with confidence.

The interaction effect also can be represented by treatment effects. To isolate these, we first need to remove the influence of the main effects from the data so that the interaction effects are not contaminated by the main effects. We illustrate the procedures for doing so using the sample data in Table 1.1 and then generalize our logic to the case of population parameters. The process involves focusing on a given cell mean (e.g., $\overline{X}_{CP,CJ}$) and literally subtracting from it the treatment effects for the levels of the main effects that define the cell. For example, the cell "Caucasian perpetrator, Caucasian juror" requires that we subtract the treatment effect for "Caucasian perpetrator" and the treatment effect for "Caucasian juror" from the cell mean:

$$\overline{X}'_{CP,CJ} = \overline{X}_{CP,CJ} - t_{CP} - t_{CJ}$$

where $\overline{X}'_{CP,CJ}$ is the "adjusted" cell mean for the "Caucasian perpetrator, Caucasian juror" cell after removing the effects of the main effects. For the data in Table 1.1, this equals

$$\overline{X}'_{CP,CJ} = 10.00 - (-1.50) - (.50) = 11.00$$

We can repeat this process for each cell of the design, which yields the set of cell means in Table 1.2. Note that each main-effect mean in this table is equal to the grand mean and that the difference in main-effect means for a given factor is zero because the influence of the main effects has been removed from the data. The means in Table 1.2 often are called *residualized means* (Rosnow & Rosenthal, 1996) because they reflect the cell means with the effects of the main effects statistically removed. We can now define the sample interaction treatment effects for each cell of the factorial design by subtracting the grand mean from the adjusted cell mean, analogous to the process of defining treatment effects for levels of the main effects. The treatment effects are

$$t_{CP,CJ} = \overline{X}'_{CP,CJ} - \overline{X}_G = 11.00 - 13.50 = -2.50$$
$$t_{CP,AJ} = \overline{X}'_{CP,AJ} - \overline{X}_G = 16.00 - 13.50 = 2.50$$
$$t_{AP,CJ} = \overline{X}'_{AP,CJ} - \overline{X}_G = 16.00 - 13.50 = 2.50$$
$$t_{AP,AJ} = \overline{X}'_{AP,AJ} - \overline{X}_G = 11.00 - 13.50 = -2.50$$

or, in population notation,

$$\tau_{CP,CJ} = \mu'_{CP,CJ} - \mu_G$$
$$\tau_{CP,AJ} = \mu'_{CP,AJ} - \mu_G$$
$$\tau_{AP,CJ} = \mu'_{AP,CJ} - \mu_G$$
$$\tau_{AP,AJ} = \mu'_{AP,AJ} - \mu_G$$

TABLE 1.2
Adjusted Cell Means for Sentence Severity Example

| | Ethnicity of Juror | | |
Ethnicity of Perpetrator	Caucasian	African American	Row Mean
Caucasian	11.00	16.00	13.50
African American	16.00	11.00	13.50
Column mean	13.50	13.50	
Grand mean = 13.50			

The treatment effects reflect the impact of the unique combination of the two independent variables on the dependent variable over and above the main effects. Of traditional interest is whether any of these population treatment effects are nonzero. For example, the effect of having the combination of an African American juror and an African American perpetrator (independent of the main effects) is to lower sentence severity, on average, by 2.50 years from the typical punishment rating. If this sample treatment effect is statistically significant, then the null hypothesis of a zero population treatment effect is deemed untenable. In a 2×2 design, the interaction treatment effects always will be of equal absolute magnitude but will vary in sign. A statistically significant F test for the interaction, therefore, indicates that all of the separate interaction treatment effects are statistically significant.

1.1.3 A Statistical Model for Classic Analysis of Variance

Some investigators prefer to think of interactions as differences between mean differences, whereas other researchers prefer to think of interactions in terms of treatment effects or the analysis of residualized means. In practice, most researchers implicitly adopt the *difference between mean differences* perspective. The classic ANOVA model describes variations in individual scores using treatment effects:

$$Y_{ijk} = \mu_G + \tau_{Aj} + \tau_{Bk} + \tau_{ABjk} + \varepsilon_{ijk} \tag{1.1}$$

where Y_{ijk} is the score on the dependent variable for individual i that is characterized by level j of the first factor and level k of the second factor, μ_G is the grand mean, τ_{Aj} is the treatment effect for level j of the first factor

(Factor A), τ_{Bk} is the treatment effect for level k of the second factor (Factor B), τ_{ABjk} is the interaction treatment effect for the levels of j and k, and ϵ is a residual term. According to this model, a person's score is an additive function of the grand mean plus the treatment effects of the factors (including their interaction) plus random error (ϵ). It is for this reason that some methodologists object to the use of the term *interaction effect* when referring to the difference between mean differences. Such a conceptualization, they argue, does not follow from the classic ANOVA model.

We agree that the analysis of the difference between mean differences does not represent an interaction effect in the statistical sense implied by the preceding model. However, many researchers have come to associate the term *interaction* with the notion of differences between mean differences, and, as we will see, the overall F test associated with a statistical interaction for the model described by Equation 1.1 yields the same result as the overall F test designed to evaluate a statistical model that views interaction as the difference between mean differences. For this reason, we use the term *interaction effect* to refer to the more global, omnibus analysis of either the interaction treatment effects or the difference between mean differences test. The conceptualizations diverge, however, in the specification of the contrasts underlying the omnibus test (in the sense to be described in the next section) and the statistical indexes that are the focus of interpretation.

Purists may object to our more general use of the term *interaction*. Some methodologists prefer the use of the term *cell mean approach* when the focus is on the difference between mean differences and use the term *interaction effects* when the focus is on interaction treatment effects or residualized means. However, we believe that the notion of an interaction as the difference between mean differences is so firmly entrenched in the research literature that we prefer to adopt a more general connotation of the term, with the more precise focus becoming evident as the investigator explicates the specific contrasts underlying the omnibus F test associated with the interaction. We return to this issue in a later section.

The traditional tests of statistical significance of the main effects and interactions in the ANOVA model are based on the assumptions that the various ϵ are independently and normally distributed with a mean of zero, that the variances of the ϵ are equal in each cell defined by the factorial design, and that the ϵ are normally distributed within each cell defined by the factorial design. We address the issue of assumption violations in Chapter 5.

1.1.4 Factorial Designs and Mean Contrasts

Differences between the two conceptualizations of interaction can be clarified by developing the general logic of mean contrasts. To apply the logic, we focus on the mean values for each cell defined by the factorial design. In the interest of pedagogy, we use notation with numerical subscripts, where the first subscript refers to a level of Factor A and the second subscript refers to a level of Factor B. In the example analyzing punishment severity, Factor A is the ethnicity of the perpetrator; Level 1 refers to the Caucasian perpetrator, and Level 2 refers to the African American perpetrator. Factor B is the ethnicity of the juror; Level 1 refers to the Caucasian juror, and Level 2 refers to the African American juror. The formula for testing the statistical significance for any given contrast is

$$t = \frac{c_1\overline{X}_{11} + c_2\overline{X}_{12} + c_3\overline{X}_{21} + c_4\overline{X}_{22}}{\sqrt{MS_{ERROR}\left(\dfrac{c_1^2}{n_{11}} + \dfrac{c_2^2}{n_{12}} + \dfrac{c_3^2}{n_{21}} + \dfrac{c_4^2}{n_{22}}\right)}} \tag{1.2}$$

where n_{jk} is the sample size for the cell defined by level j of Factor A and level k of Factor B, MS_{ERROR} is the relevant error mean square from the ANOVA summary table (MS_{WITHIN} in Table 1.1), and c is a contrast coefficient associated with each cell. We first develop the mechanics of this formula and then explore its logic in the context of factorial designs.

Focus first on the numerator of Equation 1.2. The different c coefficients are used to define a contrast between means that is of conceptual interest. Suppose, for example, that we were interested in performing a contrast that compares the mean for cell $(1, 1)$ to the mean for cell $(2, 1)$. This contrast corresponds to the effect of the ethnicity of the perpetrator, but just for Caucasian jurors, because it contrasts the mean for the Caucasian perpetrator, Caucasian juror (cell $1, 1$) to the mean for the African American perpetrator, Caucasian juror (cell $2, 1$). We want to define values of c that isolate this contrast. Suppose we set $c_1 = 1$, $c_2 = 0$, $c_3 = -1$, and $c_4 = 0$. Substituting these values into the numerator, we obtain

$$1\,\overline{X}_{11} + 0\,\overline{X}_{12} + -1\,\overline{X}_{21} + 0\,\overline{X}_{22}$$

which equals $\overline{X}_{11} - \overline{X}_{21}$, thereby isolating the contrast of interest. The values for the various terms are substituted into Equation 1.2, yielding the following:

$$t = \frac{(1)\ 10.00 + (0)\ 14.00 + (-1)\ 18.00 + (0)\ 12.00}{\sqrt{15.92\ (\frac{1^2}{20} + \frac{0^2}{20} + \frac{-1^2}{20} + \frac{0^2}{20})}}$$

$$= \frac{-8.00}{1.262} = -6.34$$

This contrast evaluates the null hypothesis that the difference $\mu_{11} - \mu_{21} = 0$ against the alternative hypothesis that $\mu_{11} - \mu_{21} \neq 0$. The resulting t value has a sampling distribution that follows a t distribution with degrees of freedom equal to the degrees of freedom associated with the mean square error ($df = 76$). In this case, the contrast is statistically significant ($p < .05$).

Equation 1.2 is quite general and typically is applied with the constraint that the sum of the cs must equal 0. Contrasts that use Equation 1.2 often are called *single degree of freedom* contrasts because when they are expressed as an F ratio (i.e., t^2), the numerator degrees of freedom always will be 1 and the denominator degrees of freedom will be those associated with MS_{ERROR}.

As another example using Equation 1.2, suppose we want to evaluate the main effect of Factor A (ethnicity of the perpetrator) by contrasting the average of cells corresponding to μ_{11} and μ_{12} with the average of cells corresponding to μ_{21} and μ_{22}. This can be accomplished using the coefficients .50, .50, −.50, and −.50 for c_1, c_2, c_3, and c_4, respectively:

$$t = \frac{(.50)\ 10.00 + (.50)\ 14.00 + (-.50)\ 18.00 + (-.50)\ 12.00}{\sqrt{15.92\ (\frac{.50^2}{20} + \frac{.50^2}{20} + \frac{-.50^2}{20} + \frac{-.50^2}{20})}}$$

$$= -3.00\ /\ .893 = -3.36$$

which is distributed as t with 76 degrees of freedom. Note that if one squares this value of t ($-3.36^2 = 11.31$), one obtains the value of the F ratio for the main effect of ethnicity of the perpetrator in the summary table in Table 1.1. Thus, there is a direct correspondence between Equation 1.2 and the F test in traditional 2×2 ANOVA.

Equation 1.2 also can be used to evaluate the interaction effect when it is conceptualized as the difference between mean differences. Suppose we chose ethnicity of the juror as the moderator variable. To examine the interaction effect, we define the coefficients so that we subtract the difference between the means for Groups 1 and 3 (representing $\overline{X}_{11}$ and $\overline{X}_{21}$

with associated c's of c_1 and c_3) from the difference between means for Groups 2 and 4 (representing $\overline{X}_{12}$ and $\overline{X}_{22}$ with associated c's of c_2 and c_4). The contrast coefficients should capture the relation of $(1-1)-(1-1)$ for $(c_1 - c_3) - (c_2 - c_4)$, which yields the c values of $c_1 = 1.0$, $c_2 = -1.0$, $c_3 = -1.0$, and $c_4 = 1.0$ after taking into account the negative sign between the two sets of parentheses:

$$t = \frac{(1)\ 10.00 + (-1)\ 14.00 + (-1)\ 18.00 + (1)\ 12.00}{\sqrt{15.92\ (\frac{1^2}{20} + \frac{-1^2}{20} + \frac{-1^2}{20} + \frac{1^2}{20})}}$$

$$= \frac{-10.00}{1.784} = -5.60$$

Again, if we square -5.60 ($-5.60^2 = 31.40$), we obtain the value of the F ratio for the interaction effect in the summary table in Table 1.1.

Finally, Equation 1.2 can be used to isolate treatment effects for the levels of either the main effect or the interaction. Simple algebra shows that the treatment effect for Level 1 of Factor A (ethnicity of the perpetrator) is isolated if $c_1 = .25$, $c_2 = .25$, $c_3 = -.25$, and $c_4 = -.25$:

$$t = \frac{(.25)\ 10.00 + (.25)\ 14.00 + (-.25)\ 18.00 + (-.25)\ 12.00}{\sqrt{15.92\ (\frac{.25^2}{20} + \frac{.25^2}{20} + \frac{-.25^2}{20} + \frac{-.25^2}{20})}}$$

$$= \frac{-1.50}{.446} = -3.36$$

Note that the absolute value of t is identical to the one we observed when we tested the main effect of Factor A by comparing the difference between marginal means for this factor. If one wants to isolate the interaction treatment effect for the combination focused on the Caucasian perpetrator coupled with a Caucasian juror, then the relevant coefficients are $c_1 = .25$, $c_2 = -.25$, $c_3 = -.25$, and $c_4 = .25$. Application of these coefficients would yield an absolute t value that is identical to the absolute t value observed when the focus is on the difference between mean differences (i.e., 5.60).

In sum, when we perform a traditional ANOVA on a set of scores, we are essentially performing a series of contrasts among the cell means that are characterized by the factorial design. The contrasts map onto either a comparison of the difference between means (e.g., the difference in means for the main effect of Factor A, the difference in means for the main effect of Factor B, the difference between mean differences in the case of an interaction) or the analysis of treatment effects, as defined by the classic ANOVA model (e.g., the treatment effect of being an African American perpetrator, the treatment effect of the unique combination of being an African American perpetrator as judged by an African American juror). A central feature of the analysis of factorial designs is deciding what contrasts one is interested in evaluating (i.e., what c values to use). In most applications that use (2×2) factorial designs, three sets of contrasts are pursued: (a) the comparison of the mean for one level of Factor A with that for another level of Factor A, (b) the comparison of the mean for one level of Factor B with that for another level of Factor B, and (c) the comparison of the difference between Factor A means at one level of Factor B with that at another level of Factor B. The first set of contrasts has come to be referred to as the *main effect of A*, the second set has come to be referred to as the *main effect of B*, and the third set, much to the chagrin of some (e.g., Rosnow & Rosenthal, 1989a), has come to be referred to as the *interaction of A and B*. No matter what label one chooses to give to a set of contrasts, the bottom line of the analysis is the act of specifying contrast coefficients that are informative, theoretically meaningful, and consistent with the underlying statistical model.

1.1.5 What to Interpret: Differences Between Mean Differences or Treatment Effects/Residualized Means?

Table 1.3 presents the mean values and treatment effects for the punishment severity study. In the former case, the row marginals contain the means for ethnicity of the perpetrator collapsing across the ethnicity of the juror. The column marginals contain the means for ethnicity of the juror collapsing across the ethnicity of the perpetrator. In the case of treatment effects, the cell values represent the treatment effects for the interaction. In a 2×2 design, these treatment effects always will be equal in absolute magnitude (but varying in sign), and there always will be a *crossover* interaction when the treatment effects are plotted. The row marginals contain the treatment effects for the levels of the ethnicity of the perpetrator factor, and the column marginals contain the treatment effects for the levels of the ethnicity of the juror factor.

At first glance, the two subtables appear to yield different conclusions. For the cell means, the tendency for Caucasian jurors to favor more lenient

TABLE 1.3
Summary of Means and Treatment Effects

Ethnicity of Perpetrator	Ethnicity of Juror		Row Mean
	Caucasian	African American	
Means			
Caucasian	10.00	14.00	12.00
African American	18.00	12.00	15.00
Column mean	14.00	13.00	
Treatment effects			
Caucasian	–2.50	2.50	–1.50
African American	2.50	–2.50	1.50
Column effect	.50	–.50	
Grand mean = 13.50			

sentences for members of their own ethnic group as opposed to members of another ethnic group ($10.00 - 18.00 = -8.00$) is much stronger than the corresponding tendency for African American jurors ($14.00 - 12.00 = 2.00$). Examining the treatment effects, however, we see that the effect of the unique combination of being a Caucasian perpetrator as evaluated by a Caucasian juror (after controlling for the main effects) is to lower punishment, on average, by –2.50 years, and this also is true for an African American perpetrator being evaluated by an African American juror. Thus, the unique joint effect of sentencing an individual of one's own ethnic group is to lower the proposed sentence, on average, 2.50 years over and above the impact of main effects, and this is true for both Caucasians and African Americans. Which characterization is correct?

The answer is that both are correct but that the two characterizations represent different things. The focus on cell means is compatible with a moderator approach in which we ask whether the effect of one variable on the dependent variable (as reflected by mean differences) changes as a function of the level of the moderator variable. The focus on treatment effects, instead, is concerned with the partitioning of individual scores into the component parts defined by Equation 1.1 with an emphasis on identifying the magnitude of the components (i.e., treatment effects) given the statistical constraints imposed by the model. In this latter method, the treatment effects for the interaction term strip away influences due to main effects and focus solely on the effects of the unique combination of two levels of the factors. By contrast, the cell means represent a summary of all of the individual components of Equation 1.1 coming together to determine a mean score.

As noted earlier, the most common orientation of researchers is to conceptualize main effects in terms of differences between means as a function of levels of the factor in question and interactions in terms of the moderator framework. Conceptually, the focus is on contrasts that define these differences, and conclusions are made relative to cell and marginal means rather than to treatment effects. The F tests for the main effects and interaction in traditional ANOVA summary tables are completely compatible with this orientation in that they map directly onto contrasts involving mean differences and differences between mean differences.

We believe that the moderator conceptualization of interaction more often maps onto questions that are of theoretical interest to the social science researcher and usually will be less awkward conceptually than the framework based on treatment effects. The vast majority of studies that use factorial designs in the social sciences pose research questions that focus on differences between mean differences, characterize interactions in terms of differences between mean differences, and draw substantive conclusions based on characterizations of differences between mean differences. This focus has served the social sciences well in terms of theory development and theory testing. This is not to say that there will never be contexts in which the focus on interaction treatment effects is of interest. However, for the types of questions posed by most researchers, the cell mean or moderator framework more often maps onto the contrasts that are of theoretical interest.

We can illustrate the conceptual orientations of the two approaches using a 2×2 factorial design with population means. The study examined the effect of administering a drug, Drug A, on depression and whether the effect of the drug differs if the patient also is taking Drug B. Depression was measured on a 30-point scale with higher scores indicating greater depression. The first factor was whether or not Drug A was prescribed for patients, and the second factor was whether or not Drug B also was prescribed for patients. Here are the population means:

	Drug B Present	Drug B Absent	Mean
Drug A Present	8.0	20.0	14.0
Drug A Absent	20.0	20.0	20.0
Mean	14.0	20.0	Grand mean = 17.0

Focusing on the interaction effect using the moderator approach, it can be seen that the presence or absence of Drug B moderates the effect of Drug A on depression. When Drug B is present, the effect of Drug A is to lower depression by 20.0 – 8.0 = 12.0. When Drug B is not present, Drug A has no effect on depression (20.0 – 20.0 = 0.0). The difference between these mean differences (12.0 – 0.0 = 12.0) captures the interaction effect and provides a direct statement about the relative effects of Drug A in the presence versus the absence of Drug B.

The analysis of cell means also provides perspectives on the effects of administering Drugs A and B simultaneously. For example, the effect of administering both drugs simultaneously relative to administering only Drug A is 8.0 – 20.0 = –12.0. The effect of administering both drugs simultaneously relative to administering just Drug B also is –12.0. The effect of administering both drugs simultaneously relative to doing nothing (i.e., relative to the control condition) is 8.0 – 20.0 = –12.0.

Now, let us examine the same data using treatment effects. We focus our interpretation on a given cell of the design, for example, the cell characterized by the presence of both Drug A and Drug B. The mean in this cell can be decomposed into four components: the grand mean (17.0) plus the treatment effect for the main effect of "Drug A present" (14.0 – 17.0 = –3.0) plus the treatment effect for the main effect of "Drug B present" (14.0 – 17.0 = –3.0) plus the treatment effect for the interaction representing the unique combination of both drugs being present (which equals –3.0). Summing the grand mean and all the treatment effects together yields the cell mean score of 8.0. The treatment effect for the second component, "Drug A present," was –3.0, suggesting that the effect of the presence of Drug A is, on average, to lower scores 3.0 points. This also is true of Drug B, where the treatment effect for "Drug B present" is –3.0. Let us examine the treatment effects for the interaction for each cell of the design:

	Drug B Present	Drug B Absent
Drug A Present	–3.0	3.0
Drug A Absent	3.0	–3.0

According to this table, the unique joint effect of doing nothing (i.e., the interaction treatment effect for the cell "Drug A Absent, Drug B Absent") is to lower depression scores 3.0 units relative to the grand mean, a characterization that seems intuitively strange (i.e., one can reduce depression, in part, by doing nothing). Also, the unique joint effect of doing nothing is identical to the unique joint effect of administering both drugs simultaneously. These statements *are* meaningful so long as one keeps in mind the nature of the parameters that are being described as dictated by Equation 1.1 and the statistical constraints imposed on the parameters. However, the parameters are not as intuitively appealing as was the case with the moderator approach. Note that we are not saying that one framework is correct and that the other framework is incorrect. We are only saying that in many contexts, the focus on cell means is an easier way in which to think about matters and more closely maps onto the types of questions that a researcher is interested in addressing.

Ultimately, the contrasts that a researcher pursues should be determined by the theory and questions that one wants to address. When we apply the analytic methods associated with ANOVA and examine F ratios, we are implicitly conducting three sets of contrasts that are "wired in" to the analysis, to use the words of Rosenthal and Rosnow (1989). From the perspective of the moderator approach, the first wired-in contrast is the difference between means for the two levels of Factor A. The second wired-in contrast is the difference between means for the two levels of Factor B. The third wired-in contrast is the difference between mean differences based on the moderator variable. From the treatment effect perspective, the first wired-in contrast is the treatment effect for the levels of Factor A, the second wired-in contrast is the treatment effect for the levels of Factor B, and the third wired-in contrast is the treatment effect for the unique combination of levels defined by Factors A and B after the treatment effects for Factors A and B have been removed. When a researcher applies the formulas for deriving the traditional summary table, we do not know which set of contrasts the researcher has in mind because the two sets yield identical F ratios. The focus of the investigator becomes clear only based on how he or she positions the contrasts on a theoretical level prior to the analysis or after the analysis has been conducted and the researcher makes the theoretical focus evident.

Yet another perspective on the two frameworks can be brought to bear for those familiar with dummy variables in multiple regression (Hardy, 1993). For the moderator or cell mean approach as applied to a 2×2 design, the main effects and interaction are represented by three dummy variables (one for the main effect of Factor A, one for the main effect of Factor B, and a product term) that use dummy coding. For the analysis of treatment effects, the same three dummy variables are used but with effect coding. Both forms of coding yield identical F ratios in terms of evaluating the statistical significance of the separate main effects and interaction. However, the regression coefficients reflect either mean differences (in the case of dummy coding) or treatment effects (in the case of effect coding). It is not the case that one coding scheme is "more correct" than the other. The coding scheme one adopts is determined by the types of contrasts that one wants the regression coefficients to reflect. We do not believe that good data-analytic practice is served by arguing that there is a correct and an incorrect way to conceptualize interactions. In the final analysis, the core issue is the specification of meaningful contrasts and interpreting those contrasts in a manner that is consistent with the substantive processes that they are presumed to reflect (Petty et al., 1996).

Rosnow and Rosenthal (1991, 1996) argue that researchers who perform traditional ANOVA calculations and then examine the difference between differences in cell means are not examining interaction effects. They state that such "cell mean" analyses are inconsistent with the underlying statistical model and urge the researcher to focus, where appropriate, on the true interaction parameters, namely the effects associated with the interaction in Equation 1.1. We would argue that analysts who rely on traditional ANOVA formulas to calculate F ratios and who then examine differences in cell means to explore interactions are acting in a way that is consistent with a moderator conceptualization of interaction and in a way that is consistent with a coherent statistical model that underlies such a conceptualization, namely the general linear model within the context of a set of guided contrasts (or the cell means model as described by Kirk, 1995). In the final analysis, we agree with Rosnow and Rosenthal (1991, 1996) that the statistical model and contrasts one uses ultimately should be those that best map onto the theoretical questions of interest.

1.2 Subsidiary Analyses and Issues

Now we consider a number of topics often associated with interaction analysis or that are central to developments in later chapters.

1.2.1 Simple Main-Effects Analysis

An analytic method frequently associated with interaction analysis is that of simple main-effects analysis. Numerous statisticians have noted that simple main-effects analysis has no necessary relationship with interaction analysis for either the moderator or residualized mean frameworks and is deficient for revealing the nature of an interaction effect (Kirk, 1995;

Marasculio & Levin, 1970). Instead, simple main-effects analysis addresses the question of whether there is a mean difference on a dependent variable as a function of an independent variable at each level of the moderator variable. For example, is there an effect of ethnicity of the perpetrator for just African American jurors? Is there an effect of the ethnicity of the perpetrator for just Caucasian jurors? These questions are answered using simple main-effects analysis. Such questions do not address the central focus of interaction analysis, namely whether the effect for African American jurors is larger or smaller than the effect for Caucasian jurors or whether there is a nonzero interaction treatment effect for the unique combination of levels of the two factors. Again, the focus of simple main-effects analysis is whether the independent variable is related to the dependent variable at each level of the moderator variable, considered separately.

Simple main-effects analysis can be executed using Equation 1.2 with appropriately defined contrasts. For example, the simple main-effect analysis to determine whether there is an effect of ethnicity of the perpetrator for just Caucasian jurors would use Equation 1.2 with the coefficients $c_1 = 1$, $c_2 = 0$, $c_3 = -1$, and $c_4 = 0$. We conducted this analysis as one of our previous examples and found it to be statistically significant.

1.2.2 The Choice of Error Terms

Equation 1.2 is a very general expression for evaluating main effects, simple main effects, and interactions in 2×2 factorial ANOVAs. The formula is applicable to designs that have all between-subject factors, all within-subject factors, or both between- and within-subject factors. In all of these designs, the individual cell means and their associated c coefficients are used in the numerator of Equation 1.2. The coefficients, cell sample sizes, and relevant mean square error are used in the denominator of Equation 1.2. For example, in a 2×2 design where the first factor is between subjects in nature and the second factor is within subjects in nature, a single degree of freedom contrast involving the main-effect means for the first factor uses the mean square error associated with the between-subject main effect. The contrast focused on the within-subject main effect uses the mean square error associated with the within-subject main effect. Contrasts involving the interaction effect use the mean square error when forming the F ratio for the interaction effect. The choice of the value of MS_{ERROR} for a simple main-effect contrast is dictated by the same considerations as those described in standard ANOVA textbooks (e.g., some simple main effects require the pooling of error terms). In addition, the formula is appropriate for both fixed- and random-effects factors so long as the appropriate error value is taken from the summary table and used for MS_{ERROR} in Equation 1.2.

We do not suggest using Equation 1.2 in place of the traditional methods for computing F ratios and evaluating main effects and interactions in 2 × 2 factorial designs. Our use of the equation is for pedagogical purposes to underscore the fact that the concepts of main effects and interactions are just mean differences resulting from a set of contrast coefficients. As will be seen in Chapter 4, Equation 1.2 also forms the foundation for decomposing more complex interactions.

1.2.3 Graphical Representations of Interactions in 2 × 2 Designs

Factorial data can be presented graphically, and such graphs have certain regularities in the presence of statistical interaction. The moderator conceptualization of interaction plots cell means, whereas the treatment effect approach plots residualized means. Figure 1.1 presents plots of cell means, and Figure 1.2 presents plots of residualized means. Figures 1.1a and 1.1b show plots of cell means when an interaction effect is present (Figure 1.1b is a plot of the severity of punishment data). The horizontal axis lists the values of the focal independent variable, the vertical axis represents the values of the dependent variable, and the dots or triangles represent the cell means for the dependent variable at each level of the independent and moderator variables. A line connects the dots or triangles for the cell means within each level of the moderator variable. Note that in both Figures 1.1a and 1.1b, the lines that result are not parallel. This can be contrasted with Figures 1.1c and 1.1d, in which an interaction effect is not present. In these latter cases, the lines are parallel. This always will be the case when there is no statistical interaction. In practice, the lines characterizing sample means rarely will be exactly parallel even when a statistically nonsignificant interaction is observed because of sampling error. However, for population data, a statistical interaction implies nonparallel lines, whereas the lack of an interaction implies parallel lines.

Some researchers characterize interactions as being either *ordinal* or *crossover* interactions. An ordinal interaction is when the two lines are not parallel but they do not intersect with one another. A crossover interaction is when the two nonparallel lines intersect. Figure 1.1a is an ordinal interaction, and Figure 1.1b is a crossover interaction.

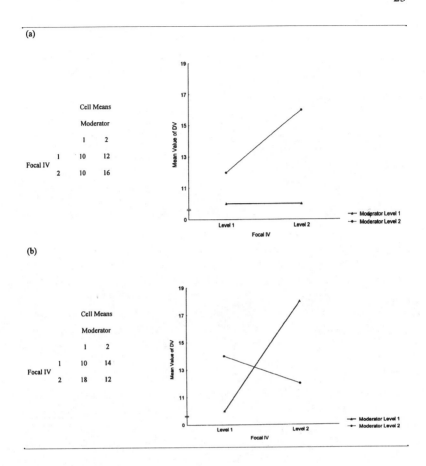

Figure 1.1a & b.   Plots of Cell Means
NOTE: DV = dependent variable; IV = independent variable.

   The graphs in Figures 1.1a and 1.1b also reveal trends in simple main-effect means. For population data, a perfectly flat (horizontal) line means that the focal independent variable has no effect on the mean values of the dependent variable at the given level of the moderator variable. This is illustrated in Figure 1.1a for Level 1 of the moderator variable. A non-horizontal line implies the presence of a simple main effect (except for sampling error), as reflected in Figure 1.1a for Level 2 of the moderator variable.

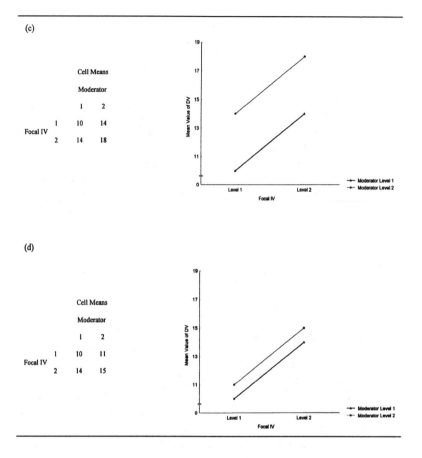

Figure 1.1c & d.   Continued

Finally, the graphical plot provides indirect information about the main-effect means. For the focal independent variable, this can best be seen by examination of Figure 1.1a. The mean value on the dependent variable at Level 1 of the focal independent variable is halfway between the two points directly above the demarcation of Level 1 on the *x* axis. The mean value on the dependent variable at Level 2 of the focal independent variable is halfway between the two points directly above the demarcation of Level 2 on the *x* axis. For the main effect of the moderator variable, the larger the difference in main-effect means, the more the lines will be separated on the

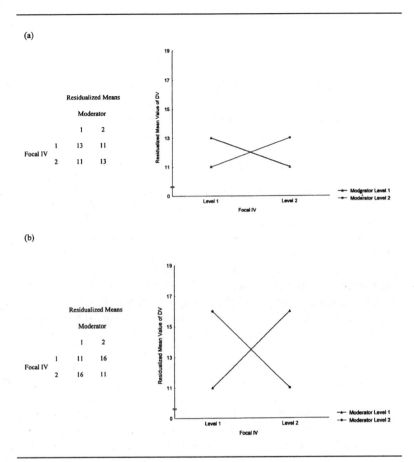

Figure 1.2 a & b. Plots of Residualized Means
NOTE: DV = dependent variable; IV = independent variable.

vertical axis, everything else being equal. Lines that are close together suggest a small main effect of the moderator variable, whereas lines that are highly separated from each other imply a large main effect, everything else being equal. For example, the lines in Figure 1.1c are more separated (i.e., farther apart) than the lines in Figure 1.1d, indicating that the main-effect mean disparaties for the moderator variable are larger in Figure 1.1c than in Figure 1.1d.

Figures 1.2a and 1.2b use the same data as do Figures 1.1a and 1.1b but plot residualized means instead of the cell means. For a 2×2 design with an interaction present, the lines always will cross over and the patterning of the residualized means always will be "X" shaped, no matter what the values of the raw cell means. The lack of an interaction is characterized by four equivalent residualized means, all of which are equal in value to the grand mean. Such a scenario is awkward to plot, and such plots typically are not generated in 2×2 designs with no statistical interaction.

1.2.4 Multiple Contrasts and Experimentwise Error Rates

The analysis of data from factorial designs typically involves more than one contrast. When a single contrast is performed, the probability of a Type I error for that contrast is the alpha level, α, which traditionally is set at .05. If more than one contrast is performed, then the probability of a Type I error for any given contrast is α (i.e., .05). However, statisticians distinguish a second type of error rate, called the *experimentwise error rate*, when many contrasts are performed. This is the probability of making at least one Type I error across the multiple contrasts. For example, the traditional 2×2 ANOVA examines three contrasts: one for the main effect of Factor A, one for the main effect of Factor B, and one for the interaction effect. For any given contrast, the *per contrast* error rate (also called the *per comparison* error rate) is the traditional .05. However, the experimentwise error rate across the three contrasts is not .05 but rather higher than this. When a set of contrasts are orthogonal, the probability of at least one Type I error occurring across the contrasts is equal to $1.0 - (1.0 - \alpha)^k$, where k is the number of contrasts. For three contrasts, this would be $1.0 - (1.0 - .05)^3 = .143$. We use α_e to refer to the probability of observing at least one Type I error across a set of contrasts.

A researcher often desires to maintain the experimentwise error rate for a set of contrasts at some specified level (e.g., $\alpha_e = .05$). Many techniques have been proposed for doing so, and these generally fall under the rubric of *multiple comparison procedures*. The choice of a multiple comparison procedure is complex and cannot be considered in detail here. For a discussion of these methods, see Kirk (1995) and Toothaker (1993). The main purpose of this subsection is to raise the issue of controlling experimentwise error rates and to comment on some misconceptions concerning the practice of doing so.

Most misconceptions concern when it is appropriate to control for the experimentwise error rate. A common belief is that procedures for controlling the experimentwise error rate should be invoked for exploratory contrasts but not for a priori or planned contrasts as dictated by a theory. Consider the following example. Two researchers conduct the identical experiment that uses a one-way design with an independent variable that has three groups. The first investigator has a theory that leads him or her to posit three a priori contrasts that correspond to comparing Group 1 to Group 2, comparing Group 1 to Group 3, and comparing Group 2 to Group 3 (i.e., the investigator plans to conduct all possible pairwise contrasts). The second investigator does not have such a theory and, instead, adopts an exploratory mode in which he or she plans to examine all possible pairwise contrasts. According to some, the first investigator would not invoke statistical procedures to control for the experimentwise error rate because his or her contrasts are "planned." However, the second investigator should invoke such controls.

Note that the only difference in the two scenarios is that the first investigator has uttered a set of words about a theory before conducting the experiment. However, "chance" does not have ears. Chance results are equally likely to occur in both situations, no matter what words come out of a person's mouth. It does not matter if the first investigator says "I have such and such a rationale for doing this particular contrast" any more than if the first investigator says "I think I will go home and eat a large dinner tonight." Chance will be operating. In our view, the central issue is not whether a set of contrasts are exploratory or guided by theory; rather, the issue is whether one desires to control the experimentwise error rate or not. Sometimes an investigator will want to control the experimentwise error rate even though all of the contrasts are theoretically motivated. Sometimes an investigator may not want to control the experimentwise error rate even though the contrasts are exploratory. A simple decision rule (e.g., "If it is a theory-based contrast, then you don't need to control for experimentwise error rates; if it is exploratory, then you do") obscures the fact that chance effects are operating in both scenarios.

The term *post hoc* often is used to characterize contrasts that are performed only after inspecting the data. Although the term *post hoc* sometimes has been associated with exploratory analyses, we view the concepts as being distinct. In exploratory analysis, the researcher does not have a strong theory guiding the analysis, but the researcher specifies *a priori* the exploratory contrasts that he or she will pursue. This was the case in the previous example for the investigator who decided to analyze all possible pairwise comparisons of means. By contrast, post hoc analyses are contrasts that are conducted based on examination of the data. For example, an investigator who conducts an experiment using a one-way design with four groups may examine the means and decide that only two of the groups exhibit a large discrepancy from each other. The investigator, therefore, conducts a single contrast comparing the two groups, ignoring the remaining pairwise comparisons. In some respects, the researcher has implicitly conducted analyses of all possible contrasts using a subjective criterion ("This difference looks large to me, but this difference does not") rather than a formal statistical criterion. Corrections for experimentwise errors in such post hoc cases can be invoked by the well-known Scheffé method (Maxwell & Delaney, 1990). For an excellent discussion of these concepts and methods for controlling experimentwise error rates, see Kirk (1995), Maxwell and Delaney (1990), and Toothaker (1993).

It is our experience that a researcher usually has a good sense of what contrasts he or she wants to examine prior to data collection. This is even true of exploratory research in which the investigator can specify a priori those contrasts that will effectively explore the range of questions that he or she is interested in addressing. As will be discussed in later chapters, we believe that such a scenario should lead the researcher to directly test the contrasts of interest with lesser concern for the evaluation of the overall omnibus null hypothesis of which the contrasts may be a subset. Effective controls of experimentwise error rates across these contrasts should be enacted, as appropriate.

A second misconception that we have encountered is that the experimentwise error rate remains at α so long as the contrasts comprising the set are orthogonal to each other (see Toothaker, 1993, for a discussion of orthogonal contrasts). This is fallacious. The experimentwise error rate becomes inflated as the number of contrasts increases, even if the contrasts are orthogonal. Although contemporary practice is not to invoke controls for experimentwise error for a priori orthogonal contrasts (see Kirk, 1995, p. 122), we believe that the decision to use such controls should not be based on the statistical property of whether a set of contrasts is orthogonal; rather, the decision should be based on the substantive and practical consequences of permitting the experimentwise error rate to exceed α across the contrasts in question. These issues are complex and subject to debate. Interested readers are referred to Duncan (1955), Ryan (1962), and Wilson (1962).

There are many methods that have been proposed for controlling experimentwise error rates. One approach is the traditional Bonferroni method, which divides the per comparison alpha level by the number of contrasts being performed. A contrast is declared statistically significant if the p value yielded by the contrast is less than this adjusted alpha level. One problem with the Bonferroni method is that it tends to have less statistical power than other approaches that effectively control the experimentwise error rate. Holm (1979) suggests a modified Bonferroni method that is more powerful than the traditional approach (see also Holland & Copenhaver, 1988, and Seaman, Levin, & Serlin, 1991) but that adequately maintains experimentwise error rates at the desired alpha level. We demonstrate the logic of the approach using the punishment severity study, controlling the experimentwise error rate at .05 across the three contrasts corresponding to the two main effects and the interaction effect. First, a p value is obtained for each contrast. The p values are then ordered from smallest to largest. Equal p values are ordered arbitrarily or by using theoretical criteria. The contrast with the smallest p value is evaluated against an alpha of $.05/k$, where k is the total number of contrasts performed (in this case 3). If this leads to rejection of the corresponding null hypothesis (because the observed p value is less than the adjusted alpha level), then the next smallest p value is tested against an alpha level of $.05/(k - 1)$, where $(k - 1)$ is the remaining number of contrasts. If this test leads to null hypothesis rejection, then the next smallest p value is tested against an alpha level of $.05/(k - 2)$ and so on until a nonsignificant difference is observed. Once a statistically nonsignificant difference is observed, all remaining contrasts are declared nonsignificant. In the present example, the p values and alpha levels are as follows:

Remaining Number of Contrasts	F Ratio	p Value	α/(Remaining Number of Contrasts)	Contrast
3	31.40	< .0001	.017	A × B
2	11.31	< .0012	.025	Main effect of A
1	1.26	< .2652	.050	Main effect of B

The main effect for Factor A (ethnicity of the perpetrator) and the interaction effect are declared statistically significant because the observed p value is less than α/(remaining number of contrasts). The main effect of Factor B (ethnicity of the juror) is not statistically significant.

Kromery and Dickinson (1995) evaluated the traditional Bonferroni method, the modified Bonferroni method, and another variant of the

Bonferroni method by Hochberg (1988) as a means of controlling experimentwise error rates across the omnibus tests of main effects and interactions in factorial ANOVA. They found that the traditional Bonferroni method lacks adequate statistical power relative to the other methods and that the Holm and Hochberg modified Bonferroni methods are superior in terms of maintaining the experimentwise error rate at .05 without sacrificing statistical power.

The control of experimentwise error rates comes at some cost. Such controls often decrease statistical power to the point where the probability of a Type II error is unacceptable. For example, suppose one analyzes data with a $3 \times 2 \times 2$ factorial design and pursues contrast analyses for all possible pairs of means for a given main effect, all possible 2×2 tables for the two-way interactions, and all possible $2 \times 2 \times 2$ subtables for the three-way interaction. The result will be 14 contrasts in which the probability of at least one Type I error occurring is well over .50. If one used a Bonferroni method to ensure that the experimentwise error rate was maintained at .05, then the statistical power would be woefully inadequate for sample sizes representative of many social science disciplines.

A common strategy used by researchers is to define "families" of contrasts in which a control for experimentwise error rates is applied within a family but not across families. A family of contrasts is simply a subgroup of contrasts in which the grouping of contrasts has been defined based on theoretically meaningful criteria. This yields a third error rate, the across-family error rate (α_F), which is the probability that at least one family will have a Type I error. Researchers typically invoke controls for experimentwise error rates within a family of contrasts but not across a family of contrasts. A common convention is to treat each effect in the factorial design (i.e., the main effect of Factor A, the main effect of Factor B, and the interaction effect) as a separate family. In the 2×2 factorial design, there is only a single contrast within each family; hence, the control of the within-family experimentwise error rate is moot. For designs with more than two levels of a factor, the issue must be addressed. In general, the grouping of contrasts into families should be guided by theoretical considerations.

In sum, a researcher must give careful thought into how to define families of contrasts and at what alpha level he or she wants to control error rates per contrast, within a family of contrasts, and across families of contrasts. If one sets α_F at .05, then by definition α and α_E will be less than this. If α_E is set at .05, then α_F will be larger than .05 and α will be less than .05. If α is set at .05, then both α_E and α_F will be larger than .05.

In the remainder of this monograph, we will use the Holm modification of the Bonferroni method to invoke control of experimentwise error rates. We choose this method because (a) it is flexible; (b) it is appropriate for all possible pairwise contrasts, selected pairwise contrasts, and nonpairwise contrasts; (c) it can be used in between- and within-subject designs for both the traditional F tests and robust counterparts of the F test (see Chapter 5); and (d) it has more statistical power than do many of its Bonferroni counterparts. There will be instances in which a method with more statistical power can be used or in which the researcher wants to construct simultaneous confidence intervals (as discussed in Chapters 2-4), and these cannot be done with the Holm procedure. For a discussion of these methods and when they might be preferred to the Holm procedure, see Kirk (1995), Maxwell and Delaney (1990), and Toothaker (1993).

1.2.5 Statistical Power of Contrasts

If one fails to reject a null hypothesis, then it is important that the statistical power of the contrast be documented so that the probability of a Type II error can be evaluated. Statistical power analysis requires that the investigator specify a minimum population value of the numerator of the contrast that he or she wants to be sure to detect. For example, when contrasting the mean punishment level for an African American perpetrator with the mean punishment level for a Caucasian perpetrator, the researcher may decide that he or she wants to be sure to reject the null hypothesis if the population mean difference between the two ethnic groups is 1 year or more. If the true mean difference is less than this, then the researcher deems that the difference is trivial and is not concerned if a Type II error occurs. In this instance, the value of "1 year" is the minimal effect size (MES) that the researcher wants to be certain to detect.

The choice of an MES is complex and often is based on theoretical or practical considerations. Cohen (1988) provides some empirical guidelines for defining MES using a standardized measure of effect size, as described later. Once the MES is specified, the statistical power of the contrast with respect to that MES can be calculated using any of a number of widely available power analysis computer programs for personal computers. Most programs do not provide power analysis for a contrast in the form of Equation 1.2. However, the programs provide the option of conducting a power analysis for the one-sample t test, and this can be used to perform the power analysis for contrasts that have the form of Equation 1.2. For the one-sample t test, the programs typically require the user to specify (a) the alpha level, (b) the sample size, (c) the MES (often called the parameter value in one sample t test programs), (d) an estimate of the population standard deviation, and (e) if the test is one-tailed or two-tailed. To conduct the power analysis for a contrast dictated by Equation 1.2, one would specify the traditional alpha of 0.05 in conjunction with a two-tailed test and the MES as derived from substantive considerations. Using a best guess estimate of the MS_{ERROR}, calculate the denominator of Equation 1.2 for the contrast (if the power analysis is conducted after data have been collected, the observed MS_{ERROR} can be used). This is the estimated standard error for the contrast. Multiply this estimated standard error by the square root of $(df_{ERROR}+1)$ and use this result as the estimate of the population standard deviation in the computer program. For the sample size, use $(df_{ERROR}+1)$. If the computer program requests df_{ERROR} instead of the sample size, use df_{ERROR} in place of $(df_{ERROR}+1)$ in the above calculations. In the punishment severity study and a MES of one year, the estimated power for the two main effects were 0.19 and for the interaction effect it was 0.08. These are low and the study should probably have been conducted with a larger sample size. Of course, the issue of a Type II error is moot for the interaction effect and the main effect of ethnicity of perpetrator because both of these contrasts were statistically significant. The computer program NQUERY, by Janet Elashoff, offers power analysis for contrasts explicitly using Equation 1.2.

The preceding procedures evaluate statistical power for any given contrast but do not evaluate statistical power in the context of corrections for experimentwise error rates. For the traditional Bonferroni method, this can be determined by conducting a power analysis for α/k, where k is the number of contrasts performed. Computation of exact power values for the modified Bonferroni test is complex. However, a crude appreciation for statistical power can be gained by calculating power estimates for α/k, then $\alpha/(k-1)$, then $\alpha/(k-2)$, and so on. These estimates are not precise and should be considered only as general guides because of the sequential or stepdown nature of the modified Bonferroni procedure.

In addition to the statistical power associated with a given contrast, Toothaker (1993) identifies two additional types of power in the multiple contrast scenario. The first is the probability of rejecting at least one false null hypothesis across a set of contrasts. The second is the probability of rejecting each false null hypothesis across a set of contrasts. For further discussion of these concepts, see Toothaker (1993).

2. MAGNITUDE ESTIMATION AND INTERVAL ESTIMATION APPROACHES

The strategy of testing null and alternative hypotheses using the traditional p value approach has been criticized by numerous statisticians. In this chapter, we briefly note some of the objections that have been raised to the classical approach and then consider strategies that have been suggested to replace or supplement such analyses. These approaches are relevant not only to the analysis of interaction effects in factorial analysis of variance (ANOVA) but also to the analysis of any set of contrasts that uses Equation 1.2.

2.1 Criticisms of Null Hypothesis Testing

Classic null hypothesis testing has been criticized on several grounds. Cohen (1994) and others (e.g., Gigerenzer, 1993; Meehl, 1990a) note that the classic hypothesis-testing framework estimates the conditional probability of observing a certain pattern of data (e.g., a t value of 2.90 or larger) given that the null hypothesis is true, that is, $p(D|H_0)$, where D are the "data" that were observed in the study and H_0 is the null hypothesis. By contrast, the primary interest of the investigator is a different conditional probability, namely the probability that the null hypothesis is true given a certain pattern of data, that is, $p(H_0|D)$. Cohen (1994) notes that these two conditional probabilities are not always equal and provides several illustrations in the context of null hypothesis testing where the former can differ substantially from the latter. In short, critics contend that classic null hypothesis testing addresses the wrong question by estimating an inappropriate conditional probability.

A second objection to classic hypothesis-testing methods is the fact that the p values that are acted on for purposes of rejecting or failing to reject the null hypothesis are influenced by the sample sizes used in experiments. Everything else being equal, the larger the sample size, the lower the p value that one will observe and the greater the probability of rejecting the null hypothesis. According to critics, this suggests that conclusions are driven largely by the sample sizes that happen to be used in scientific studies. How valuable would the hypothesis-testing approach be if all of our experiments were conducted with a minimum of 10,000 subjects? Under this scenario, almost all experiments would yield statistically significant results, and we would be overwhelmed by a huge number of contradictory, "statistically significant" results.

A third objection to classic hypothesis testing derives from the argument by some that the null hypothesis of exact mean equivalence almost never is false and that there always will be a population mean difference between groups if one carries the result to enough decimal places. Given that the null hypothesis of exact equivalence between groups never is false, why do we insist on using statistics to determine whether we can reject a hypothesis that we know is inherently false to begin with?

A detailed consideration of these objections is beyond the scope of this monograph, and interested readers are referred to Chow (1988, 1989), Cohen (1994; see also rejoinders), Cortina and Dunlap (1997), Folger (1989), Gigerenzer (1993), Meehl (1990a, 1990b), and the series of articles introduced by Shrout (1997). Because we believe that the concerns are valid in some (but not all) contexts, we develop in this chapter methods of analysis that do not rely on the traditional hypothesis-testing framework. At least three approaches have been advocated: (a) an approach based on evaluating magnitude of effects, (b) an approach based on interval estimation, and (c) Bayesian approaches. We consider only the first two approaches because implementing the Bayesian method is complex and best considered in more detailed texts (see Phillips, 1973; Pollard, 1985).

2.2 Magnitude Estimation Approaches

Magnitude estimation approaches emphasize the importance of describing the size of the effect of an independent variable (or an interaction) on a dependent variable. A researcher often distinguishes between statistical significance and practical significance. Statistical significance refers to the case in which the null hypothesis has been rejected. In such cases, we can say with some confidence that an effect is present, but we cannot make formal statements about the size or magnitude of the effect. Scenarios occur in which the results of a test can be statistically significant (i.e., an effect is present) but the practical significance of the effect is minimal (i.e., the size of the effect is trivial). Magnitude estimation approaches focus attention on both the practical and statistical significance of an effect.

Application of the magnitude estimation framework requires that the investigator specify a priori an effect size that differentiates a trivial effect from a meaningful effect. If the effect size observed in the study is less than the criterion for meaningfulness, then the result is deemed nonsignificant even if the null hypothesis is rejected and the p value for the analysis is less than α. A researcher using this approach must provide a clear rationale for the choice of the "critical" effect size that is used to determine whether an effect should be taken seriously or ignored. This enterprise is not entirely foreign to those who use traditional hypothesis testing because specification of such critical effect sizes forms the cornerstone of statistical power analysis. Some analysts combine the effect size estimation approach with the classic hypothesis-testing approach; if a traditional test of null and alternative hypotheses is statistically significant, then an index of effect size is computed and evaluated against a critical effect size. If the hypothesis test is not statistically significant, then the issue of the size of the effect is moot because the data are not sufficient for us to reasonably conclude that the effect size is nonzero. We return to the issue of specifying a critical effect size later.

Many different indexes of effect size have been proposed. Maxwell and Delaney (1990) distinguish two general classes of measures: (a) measures of strength of effect and (b) measures of association. We consider examples of each for the 2×2 factorial design.

2.2.1 Difference in Raw Means

One index of strength of effect is simply the magnitude of the numerator of the contrast being evaluated in Equation 1.2. In the context of interaction analyses, this would be either the size of the difference between mean differences or the sizes of the interaction treatment effects. This measure of effect size is most useful when the dependent variable has a metric that is inherently meaningful or that has acquired meaning through repeated use in past research. For example, suppose that a researcher examined gender differences in annual starting salaries for African Americans as opposed to Caucasians. Suppose further that the gender difference for African Americans was such that males make, on average, $10,000 more than females, whereas the corresponding gender difference for Caucasians was $2,000, yielding a difference between mean differences of $8,000. This result suggests that a larger gender gap in annual incomes exists for African Americans than for Caucasians. The $8,000 difference is meaningful to us because we have widespread experience with money in units of dollars, we have implicit knowledge about the purchasing power of $8,000 and what the social and economic implications are of an $8,000 differential salary, and we have some sense for the distribution of incomes in the general population.

Now consider the same contrast but for a dependent variable that measures a personality trait (e.g., sociability). If we use a sociability measure that ranges from 0 to 100 and we are informed that the gender difference in sociability for African Americans is –5.5 as compared to –8.5 for Caucasians, then this statement does not have immediate intuitive meaning in terms of interpreting the magnitude of the interaction effect.

2.2.2 Standardized Mean Difference

One strategy for circumventing this interpretational difficulty is to use a standardized measure of mean difference as an index of strength of the effect. One of the most commonly used indexes is the d statistic, which typically has been explicated in the context of comparing two means (Cohen, 1988). In terms of population parameters, d is defined as

$$\delta = \frac{\mu_1 - \mu_2}{\sigma} \qquad (2.1)$$

where μ_1 is the mean for Group 1, μ_2 is the mean for Group 2, and σ is the standard deviation of scores in each of the populations (which are assumed to be equal). Equation 2.1 quantifies how much larger or smaller the mean difference is than the population standard deviation. If $\delta = 1.0$, then the mean difference is equal to the standard deviation. If $\delta = .50$, then the mean difference is half the size of the standard deviation. If $\delta = 2.0$, then the mean difference is twice the size of the standard deviation.

Equation 2.1 is readily applied to interaction effects by substituting the difference between mean differences in the numerator for $\mu_1 - \mu_2$. Suppose, for example, that the gender differences in sociability referred to earlier for African Americans and Caucasians yielded a δ of $[(-5.5) - (-8.5)] / 1.5 = 2.0$. In this case, the difference in effects is twice as large as the variability within a population.

The formula for δ is roughly analogous to the formula for a standard score, $(X - \mu) / \sigma$, where the numerator is the discrepancy between a raw score and the mean and the denominator is the standard deviation. For δ, however, the numerator is the discrepancy between means as defined by the numerator of Equation 1.2 using population parameters. Thus, just as a standard score reflects the number of standard deviations that a score is above or below the mean, δ is the number of standard deviations that a mean difference is above or below zero.

Cohen (1988) provides an extended discussion of δ for purposes of defining small, medium, and large effect sizes. For purposes of examining mean differences, he suggests that a δ of .20 represents a small effect size, a δ of .50 represents a medium effect size, and a δ of .80 represents a large effect size. Cohen acknowledges that these guidelines are somewhat arbitrary and can be revised upward or downward depending on the substantive application.

A sample estimate of δ in the context of an ANOVA is

$$d = \frac{MD}{\sqrt{MS_{ERROR}}} \tag{2.2}$$

where MD = the sample mean difference in question (i.e., the numerator of Equation 1.2) and MS_{ERROR} is the error term from the ANOVA summary table that is relevant to the contrast in question (i.e., the MS_{ERROR} in the denominator of Equation 1.2). The use of MS_{ERROR} derives from the fact that the mean square error in traditional ANOVA is a pooled within-group variance estimate across the different experimental conditions. When the MS_{ERROR} from a factorial design is used as per Equation 2.2, d is analogous to a "partial d" in the sense that it is the effect size for a contrast, holding constant all other factors in the experimental design (a concept that is discussed in greater depth in the next section).[3] Equation 2.2 can be applied to either the interpretation of mean differences or the interpretation of treatment effects. As an example, for the analysis of punishment severity ratings, the value of d for the interaction effect when the focus is on the difference between mean differences is –2.51. Thus, the difference between mean differences is more than $2\frac{1}{2}$ standard deviation units of the severity ratings. The absolute value of d for the interaction treatment effect was 0.63, or approximately two thirds of 1 standard deviation of the punishment severity ratings. The effect of the unique combination of any given cell (in terms of interaction treatment effects) was to raise or lower (depending on the sign of the treatment effect) an individual's severity rating, on average, by about two thirds of 1 standard deviation unit.

2.2.3 Percentage of Variance Accounted For

An effect size measure that provides an index of association is the percentage of variation in the dependent variable that is associated with the independent variable in question. A commonly used index is a statistic called *eta squared* (or *R squared* in many computer packages), which reflects the proportion of "explained" variance in the sample data that is attributable to an independent variable. When multiplied by 100, it yields an index of percentage of explained variance.

For between-subject designs, the eta squared associated with an effect is

$$\text{Eta}^2 = \frac{SS_{\text{EFFECT}}}{SS_{\text{TOTAL}}} \qquad (2.3)$$

where SS_{EFFECT} is the sum of squares associated with the contrast in question. For the interaction effect in the punishment severity example, eta squared is 500 / 1,910 = .26 (see Table 1.1), indicating that 26% of the variation in punishment severity ratings is associated with the interaction effect. For the main effect of ethnicity of the perpetrator, eta squared is 180 / 1,910 = .09. For the ethnicity of the juror, eta squared is .01.[4]

A second index of eta squared is called *partial eta squared*. This is the proportion of variation associated with a factor, holding constant all other factors in the design. Suppose that two investigators conducted the same experiment in which they were examining the effects of gender and attractiveness of a solicitor on the amount of money that a person donates to a charity. The attractiveness of the solicitor is manipulated by having a professional makeup artist alter the facial features of the solicitor to yield an "attractive" versus "unattractive" appearance. Suppose that the attractiveness of the solicitor is, in fact, important in influencing the amount of money donated but that the degree of attractiveness that is manipulated is different in the two studies. The first investigator, Investigator A, uses a weaker manipulation of attraction than does the second investigator, Investigator B. In the context of analyzing their respective data, the investigators observe statistically significant effects for gender and statistically significant effects of the attractiveness of the solicitor. In this case, when calculating the eta squared for gender, the eta squared will be larger for Investigator A than for Investigator B, everything else being equal. As seen in Equation 2.3, eta squared becomes smaller when the SS_{EFFECT} is constant and the SS_{TOTAL} increases in magnitude. Because Investigator B used a stronger manipulation of attractiveness than did Investigator A, this will create more variability in the dependent variable as compared to that with Investigator A. The result will be a larger SS_{TOTAL}, thereby reducing the value of eta squared for gender (assuming that the sum of squares for the effect of gender is the same in the two experiments). To circumvent such ambiguities, methodologists have proposed the index of partial eta squared, which examines the proportion of variance associated with an effect after removing the variability due to the other effects in the design from the total variability:

$$\text{Partial Eta}^2 = \frac{SS_{\text{EFFECT}}}{SS_{\text{EFFECT}} + SS_{\text{ERROR}}} \qquad (2.4)$$

where SS_{ERROR} is the sum of squares associated with the residual term for the effect (e.g., SS_{WITHIN} for a completely between-subject factorial design). For the interaction effect in the punishment severity example, the partial eta squared is 500 / (500 + 1,210) = .29. Note that because $SS_{\text{TOTAL}} = SS_A + SS_B + SS_{A \times B} + SS_{\text{ERROR}}$, the denominator of Equation 2.4 represents the total variability but with the variability due to Factors A and B (SS_A and SS_B) removed. We can summarize the eta squared and partial eta squared for each effect in the punishment severity example as follows:

Source	Eta Squared	Partial Eta Squared
Ethnicity of perpetrator (A)	.09	.13
Ethnicity of juror (B)	.01	.02
A × B	.26	.29

Although both the eta squared and partial eta squared statistics are informative, most methodologists prefer to focus on partial eta squared because it reflects an index of effect size when the other factors in the design are statistically controlled.

Effect size indexes other than those discussed here have been proposed (e.g., Anderson, 1982; Feingold, 1995; McGraw & Wong, 1992; Rosenthal 1994, 1995), but the preceding indexes represent those that are among the more commonly employed.

2.2.4 Unbiased Estimators

All of the standardized effect size indexes described heretofore are biased estimators of their corresponding population parameters with the bias being in the direction of overestimating the effect size. The degree of bias tends to decrease as the sample size increases and as the magnitude of explained variance in the population increases. Modifications to the preceding formulas have been suggested to provide approximately unbiased estimates (see Kirk, 1995, p. 180). One of the more popular indexes of association that invokes such a modification is omega squared.[5] These modifications are not necessarily desirable. For example, under some circumstances, the modification can produce an estimate that is less than zero, which is theoretically nonsensical for an index of proportion of explained variance. The usual practice is to set such estimates to zero. But adopting this practice results in a biased estimator, which is what one is trying to avoid in the first place. In addition, (nearly) unbiased estimators sometimes exhibit larger sample-to-sample fluctuations (i.e., larger standard errors) than do their biased counterparts, which also is undesirable. The issue of which sample estimator to use is complex, and we cannot make an informed, universal recommendation at this time.

An approximately unbiased estimator of δ has been developed by Hedges and Olkin (1984) and can be expressed as follows:

$$d = \{1 - [3 / (4N - 9)]\}d \tag{2.5}$$

where d is defined as in Equation 2.2 and N is the total sample size. In the study on punishment severity ratings, the value of d for the interaction effect in terms of the difference between mean differences was -2.51. The approximately unbiased estimate of δ is therefore $\{1 - [3 / ((4)(80) - 9)]\}(-2.51) = -2.49$. Fowler (1988) proposes an alternative adjustment to that proposed by Hedges and Olkin:

$$d = [(2N - 5)d] / (2N - 4)$$

The results for this estimator and that proposed by Hedges and Olkin (1984) tend to be quite similar except for the case of small sample sizes. However, Fowler suggests caution when applying his adjustment in cases where δ is outside the range of .25 to 1.50. Readers are urged to consult Fowler (1988) for additional perspectives on the use of the two estimators.

Fowler (1985) finds that a statistic called *epsilon squared* yields an approximately unbiased estimate of the population parameter for proportion of explained variance and that epsilon squared is not as conservative as the more popular omega squared. Epsilon squared can be calculated for a given contrast defined by Equation 1.2 using the following formula (Maxwell, Camp, & Arvey, 1981):

$$\text{Epsilon}^2 = \frac{\text{SS}_{\text{EFFECT}} - \text{MS}_{\text{ERROR}}}{\text{SS}_{\text{TOTAL}}}$$

For example, the value of epsilon squared for the interaction effect in the punishment severity study is $(500 - 15.92) / 1,910 = .253$.

An approximately unbiased estimate of the proportion of explained variance after partialling out the effects of the other factors in the design can be calculated from the F ratio for a given effect from the ANOVA summary table (Fowler, 1985). It is

$$\text{Partial Epsilon}^2 = (F - 1) / (F + df_{\text{ERROR}} / df_{\text{EFFECT}}) \qquad (2.6)$$

where F is the F ratio for the contrast in question (which is simply t^2 when Equation 1.2 is used), df_{ERROR} is the degrees of freedom associated with the error term for the contrast, and df_{EFFECT} is the degrees of freedom associated with the effect (which is always 1.0 when Equation 1.2 is applied). For example, the partial epsilon squared for the interaction effect in the study on punishment severity is $(31.40 - 1) / (31.40 + 76 / 1) = .283$.

In general, when the true proportion of explained variance in the population is .10 or greater and $N > 80$, there will be only minor differences between eta squared and epsilon squared for single degree of freedom contrasts. However, for smaller N, the bias in eta squared may reach unacceptable levels (see Fowler, 1985, for a more detailed discussion of this issue). We adopt the practice of using (partial) epsilon squared and setting it to zero if the formula for calculating it yields a value less than zero.

2.2.5 Criticisms of Indexes of Effect Size

Several methodologists have noted difficulties with indexes of effect size. We consider most of these issues in the context of eta squared, but they are germane to all of the "standardized" or "common metric" measures of effect size.

One criticism is that the magnitude of effect sizes is arbitrary given that the metric of the dependent variable frequently is arbitrary. Suppose that an investigator develops a scale that measures self-esteem and uses a 20-item test that sums the responses to items. Ideally, the distribution of the scores on the test should reflect the true underlying distribution of actual self-esteem. Suppose that the researcher believes that the distribution of true self-esteem is normal. If the observed scores are not normally distributed, then one might question the metric that has been established. The researcher might therefore pursue a transformation of the scores so that they better approximate a normal distribution, thus providing a better map onto the true distribution of self-esteem. In this case, the initial metric is noninterval in nature, and the transformation is applied in the attempt to produce a measure that is a linear function of the underlying dimension (i.e., that has interval-level characteristics).

Many of the measures used in the social sciences are of this nature (e.g., the metric is a function of the sum of multiple items designed to map onto an underlying dimension). Usually the measure is monotonically related to the underlying construct, but we are uncertain whether the measure is a linear function of it. A monotonic transformation of the data is thus plausible in a large number of instances. The investigator who uses the sum of a set of items has no more justification for saying his or her measure is a linear function of the underlying construct than does the investigator who uses, say, the log of the sum of the items. One criticism of effect size indexes is that they are influenced by such metrical considerations (i.e., by certain types of transformations). Thus, the value of the effect size index may be different depending on whether one analyzes raw scores or certain types of transformed scores.

The issue of metric assumptions, like many of those we will discuss, does not represent an inherent shortcoming of effect size approaches. One might argue, instead, that the source of the problem is our measurement procedures and the fact that many of our measures are not interval in character. The issue would be irrelevant if this measurement "problem" could be solved. The fact is, however, that the effect size indexes described so far assume interval-level data and that deviations from this can bias the magnitude of the estimates. Although there have been studies of the robustness of statistical tests of a null hypothesis to violations of the equal interval assumption, the issue has been investigated much less in the context of bias for indexes of effect size. We return to this issue in Chapter 5.

A second criticism of effect size approaches is that the degree to which an independent variable is manipulated frequently is arbitrary, and this also affects the value of the effect size. For example, in studies of dissonance theory, one issue that has been explored is how the degree of suffering that people willingly endure biases or influences one's attitude toward engaging in some activity related to that suffering. In one study, suffering was manipulated by having female subjects read sexually explicit materials to male experimenters. In another study, degree of suffering was manipulated by the strength of the electric shock delivered to female subjects. In neither study do we know to what extent suffering was truly manipulated. (Manipulation checks typically are used only to demonstrate that the manipulation was effective in producing *some* variability, not to measure *how much* variability.) The magnitude of the effect size in the two studies will differ if one of the studies creates more variability in the independent variable than does the other, everything else being equal. Again, the magnitude of the effect size often is arbitrary because the extent to which the independent variable is manipulated often is arbitrary.[6]

A third criticism of standardized effect size measures is that they sometimes make minuscule effects appear large and make large effects appear small. For example, if the amount of variability in the dependent variable is small, then even a small mean difference between two groups may produce an extremely large value of eta squared or delta. On the other hand, many researchers are quick to dismiss effects that account for "only" 3% to 5% of the variance in the dependent variable despite the fact that such effect sizes can be of great practical import. Many phenomena that social scientists study are determined by a complex array of multiple variables. Finding a single variable that accounts for "only" 3% to 5% of the variance is rather remarkable given this multivariate character of outcomes.

Yeaton and Sechrest (1981) provide examples that graphically illustrate the preceding limitations. As one example, they describe a study by Gastorf (1980) that found a 3.85-minute mean difference in arrival time for an appointment between individuals who have a Type A personality versus those who have a Type B personality ($p < .05$). An index of percentage of variance accounted for suggested that the Type A versus Type B distinction accounted for approximately 1.5% of the variance in arrival times. Most researchers would dismiss this as a trivial effect size. However, Yeaton and Sechrest (1981) note that if a company that employed 1,000 people experienced a 3.85-minute arrival delay for each worker over the course of a year, the result would be a loss of approximately $140,000, assuming a wage of $10 per hour. For additional discussions of cases in which small effect sizes reflect important outcomes, see Prentice and Miller (1992) and Rosenthal (1995).

Yeaton and Sechrest (1981) also characterize a scenario in which a new policy implemented by a company results in people arriving 30 seconds earlier, on average. If the variation in arrival time is small to begin with (i.e., the variance on the dependent variable is small), then the prepolicy versus postpolicy manipulation may account for large amounts of variance in arrival times (e.g., the eta squared might be .50 or greater). Aggregated across the 1,000 employees, the net savings would be only about $18,000 per year. This scenario, in which a large value of eta squared (.50) was observed, stands in stark contrast to the previous scenario, in which a small eta squared (.015) was observed relative to the ultimate dollar cost/savings for the company. Rosenthal (1995) and Abelson (1985, 1995) also provide interesting perspectives on this issue.

A related criticism of magnitude estimation approaches is the failure of researchers to adequately define and justify what constitutes trivial, small, medium, and large effect sizes. Proponents of magnitude estimation methodology often caution that a statistically significant result may not be of practical significance and state that effect size indexes help to reveal such scenarios. However, it is rare to find a detailed and rational definition of an effect size value that is to be used to define a trivial effect. The most common practice for researchers is to cite the discussion by Cohen (1988) and to use the standards for small, medium, and large effect sizes that he proposes.[7] However, Cohen is careful to point out that his guidelines are only rough approximations that could be shifted upward or downward depending on the substantive question being addressed. If we are to take magnitude estimation approaches seriously, then researchers must offer carefully considered rationales for what constitutes a trivial effect size, taking both practical (e.g., cost in dollars) and statistical (e.g., the amount of variance on the dependent variable) considerations into account.

A fifth criticism of magnitude estimation methods is that they typically (but not always) rely on point estimates of population parameters. There is a tendency for researchers to interpret effect size indexes without regard to the sampling error that is inherent in such indexes and the recognition that some indexes can be ill behaved for small samples. Indeed, the estimation of standard errors for measures of percentage of variance accounted for is difficult and of questionable utility (Fowler, 1985). Instead of characterizing effect size in terms of a single "guess" about the value of the population parameter, a more productive approach, according to critics, is to specify a range of effect sizes within which one is confident that the true effect size resides. We discuss such an approach in the next section. Suffice it to say that most researchers who report effect sizes do so in the context of a single point estimate and fail to take into account the fact that the sample size used in the study may be too small to have much confidence in the point estimate.

A final criticism of measures of effect size is that they often are assessed in the context of fixed-effects ANOVA but then are used as if they were derived from a random effects model. With fixed-effects ANOVA, one does not generalize (or should only do so with great caution) beyond the particular levels used to represent an independent variable. However, it is not uncommon for a researcher to select respondents based on, say, three levels of social class, conduct a fixed-effects ANOVA on a dependent variable, and then report effect size indexes that are interpreted to reflect the degree of association between social class in general and the dependent variable. Technically, characterizations should be made only with respect to the three levels of social class chosen for inclusion in the study. The magnitude of the effect size index might be quite different if another researcher selects three different levels of social class. Fixed-effects models and designs too often are characterized as if they were based on random effects methodology.

In sum, magnitude estimation approaches can offer useful perspectives on the relationships between variables and the effects that a factor has on a dependent variable. However, researchers often fail to appreciate subtleties in their interpretations. Use of the approach, like any approach to data analysis, requires careful thought about the substantive, practical, statistical, and measurement features of a study.

2.3 Interval Estimation Approaches

Another alternative or supplemental method to hypothesis testing is that of interval estimation. This approach identifies a population parameter of interest and then specifies an interval or range of values within which the investigator has a high degree of confidence that the population parameter falls. For example, in the study on punishment severity, the parameter of interest might be the value of the difference between population mean differences for ethnicity of the perpetrator as a function of the ethnicity of the juror, that is, the value of $(\mu_{CP,CJ} - \mu_{AP,CJ}) - (\mu_{CP,AJ} - \mu_{AP,AJ})$. This parameter represents the interaction effect in terms of differences between mean differences. In the interval estimation approach, we want to specify a range of values for the severity ratings that we can have a high degree of confidence contains the true value of this parameter.

One strategy is to calculate 95% confidence intervals about this parameter using traditional confidence interval methodology. We can use Equation 1.2 to accomplish this. The numerator of the equation specifies the sample value of the parameter of interest, using contrast coefficients:

$$\text{Parameter Estimate} = c_1\overline{X}_{11} + c_2\overline{X}_{12} + c_3\overline{X}_{21} + c_4\overline{X}_{22} \qquad (2.7)$$

In the case of the interaction contrast described earlier, the values are

Parameter Estimate = (1)10.00 + (−1)14.00 + (−1)18.00 + (1)12.00,

where the c's are defined using the logic described earlier.

The estimated standard error of the parameter is the denominator of Equation 1.2:

$$SE = \sqrt{MS_{ERROR}\left(\frac{c_1^2}{n_{11}} + \frac{c_2^2}{n_{12}} + \frac{c_3^2}{n_{21}} + \frac{c_4^2}{n_{22}}\right)} \qquad (2.8)$$

which in this case equals

$$SE = \sqrt{15.92\left(\frac{1^2}{20} + \frac{-1^2}{20} + \frac{-1^2}{20} + \frac{1^2}{20}\right)}$$

$$= 1.784$$

The 95% confidence interval is

$$CI_{.95} = \text{Parameter Estimate} \pm (SE)(t_{CRITICAL}) \qquad (2.9)$$

where $t_{CRITICAL}$ is a t value based on an alpha level of .05 from a t distribution with degrees of freedom equal to the degrees of freedom for the MS_{ERROR} in Equation 2.8. In the punishment severity case, the $df = 76$ and the critical value of t is 1.99. This yields the interval of −10.00 ± 3.55 or −13.55 to −6.45. Thus, we are reasonably confident that the true value of the population parameter is between −13.55 and −6.45.[8]

Equation 2.9 can be used to construct confidence intervals for any contrast defined by the c coefficients. Thus, it is possible to specify confidence limits for any main effect, any simple main effect, or any treatment effect by specifying the appropriate c coefficients. For example, the confidence limits for the interaction treatment effect for the "Caucasian perpetrator, Caucasian juror" cell is

Parameter Estimate = (.25)10.00 + (−.25)14.00 + (−.25)18.00 + (.25)12.00

$$SE = \sqrt{15.92\left(\frac{.25^2}{20} + \frac{-.25^2}{20} + \frac{-.25^2}{20} + \frac{.25^2}{20}\right)}$$

$$CI_{.95} = -2.50 \pm (.446)(1.99)$$
$$= -3.38 \text{ to } -1.61$$

It is possible to combine the interval estimation approach with magnitude estimation approaches by forming confidence intervals for indexes of effect size. For example, Fowler (1985; also personal communication, December 1996) describes a method for computing confidence intervals for partial epsilon squared as derived from t or F tests. We illustrate the approach using the interaction effect from the punishment severity study, as conceptualized in terms of differences between mean differences. Recall that this contrast was operationalized as follows:

$$t = \frac{(1)\,10.00 + (-1)\,14.00 + (-1)\,18.00 + (1)\,12.00}{\sqrt{15.92\,(\frac{1^2}{20} + \frac{-1^2}{20} + \frac{-1^2}{20} + \frac{1^2}{20})}}$$

$$= \frac{-10.00}{1.784} = -5.60.$$

Squaring the value of t yields the F ratio of 31.40, which is what is found in the summary table in Table 1.1. We begin by calculating an intermediate statistic called L, which is defined as

$$L = .50[(w)(x) + z_{\text{CRITICAL}}^2(x + C) - 2df_{\text{EFFECT}} + C]$$

where $w = 2df_{\text{ERROR}} - 1$, $x = df_{\text{EFFECT}}F / df_{\text{ERROR}}$, z_{CRITICAL} is the standard normal score corresponding to the two tailed alpha of interest and $C = (df_{\text{EFFECT}} + 2Nx) / (df_{\text{EFFECT}} + Nx)$. Note that when calculating x, F is the F ratio for the contrast; when calculating C, N is set equal to $df_{\text{EFFECT}} + df_{\text{ERROR}} + 1$. In the present example,

$w = (2)(76) - 1 = 151$
$x = (1)(31.40) / 76 = .413$
$N = 1 + 76 + 1 = 78$
$C = [1 + (2)(78)(.413)] / [1 + (78)(.413)] = 1.970$
$L = .50[(151)(.413) + (1.96^2)(.413 + 1.970) - (2)(1) + 1.970] = 35.763$

Once L is computed, Fowler (1985) recommends calculating the lower limit using a reiterated value of L as follows:

$$L' = L - z_{\text{CRITICAL}} \left[\sqrt{[(w)(x)(x + C)]}\right]$$

$$= 35.763 - 1.96 \ \sqrt{[(151)(.413)(.413 + 1.970)]} = 11.861$$

$$C' = (df_{\text{EFFECT}} + 2L') / (df_{\text{EFFECT}} + L') = [1 + (2)(11.861)] / (1 + 11.861) = 1.922$$

and using this new value of C', we recalculate L as

$$L_{\text{REVISED}} = .50 \ [(w)(x) + z_{\text{CRITICAL}}^{2}(x + C') - 2df_{\text{EFFECT}} + C']$$

$$= .50[(151)(.413) + (1.96^2)(.413 + 1.922) - (2)(1) + 1.922] = 35.648$$

The lower limit is

$$\text{Lower Limit} = \text{Lower } L \ / \ (\text{Lower } L + N)$$

where

$$\text{Lower } L = L_{\text{REVISED}} - z_{\text{CRITICAL}}\sqrt{[(w)(x)(x + C')]}$$

$$= 35.648 - 1.96 \ [\ \sqrt{[(151)(.413)(.413 + 1.922)]} = 11.986$$

yielding

$$\text{Lower Limit} = 11.986 \ / \ (11.986 + 78) = .133$$

These steps are then repeated for estimating the upper limit as follows:

$$L = .50[(w)(x) + z_{\text{CRITICAL}}^{2}(x + C) - 2df_{\text{EFFECT}} + C]$$

$$= .50 \ [(151)(.413) + (1.96^2)(.413 + 1.970) - (2)(1) + 1.970] = 35.763$$

The reiterated value of L is

$$L' = L + z_{\text{CRITICAL}} \ \sqrt{[(w)(x)(x + C)]}$$

$$= 35.763 + 1.96 \ \sqrt{[(151)(.413)(.413 + 1.970)]} = 59.665$$

$$C' = (df_{\text{EFFECT}} + 2L') / (df_{\text{EFFECT}} + L') = [1 + (2)(59.665)] / (1 + 59.665) = 1.984$$

and using this new value of C', we recalculate L as

$$L_{\text{REVISED}} = .50\,[(w)(x) + z_{\text{CRITICAL}}^{2}(x + C') - 2df_{\text{EFFECT}} + C']$$

$$= .50\,[(151)(.413) + (1.96^{2})(.413 + 1.984) - (2)(1) + 1.984] = 35.796$$

The upper limit is

$$\text{Upper Limit} = \text{Upper } L / (\text{Upper } L + N)$$

where

$$\text{Upper } L = L_{\text{REVISED}} + z_{\text{CRITICAL}}\sqrt{[(w)(x)(x + C')]}$$

$$= 35.796 + 1.96\,\sqrt{[(151)(.413)(.413 + 1.984)]} = 59.766$$

yielding

$$\text{Upper Limit} = 59.766 / (59.766 + 78) = .434$$

The partial epsilon squared in the sample data was .28 (applying Equation 2.6), which is our point estimate. We have a high degree of confidence that the population value of the partial proportion of explained variance is between .13 and .43. If the F ratio (or t ratio when Equation 1.2 is used) is statistically nonsignificant, then the lower limit of the interval is set to zero.

This method for interval estimation of partial eta squared developed by Fowler (1984) is algebraically cumbersome but computationally straightforward by hand calculator. It uses an approximation strategy that tends to be less accurate for F ratios with small degrees of freedom and for small effect sizes. It is possible to use computers to obtain more exact approximations, but the procedures involved are computationally intense. We believe that the approximation presented here is sufficient for most applications in the social sciences in that it will provide a reasonable sense of a range of plausible values for the population value of partial eta squared. Readers interested in developing more exact solutions are referred to the series of articles by Fowler (1984, 1985, 1986) and Tang (1938).

Fowler (1985) suggests that if a point estimate of the explained variance is to be provided, then one might consider an alternative to epsilon squared, namely the value yielded by the preceding calculations when $z_{CRITICAL}$ is set to zero. The result is an estimate of the proportion of explained variance that is at the 50th percentile or the median of its sampling distribution. The median may be preferable because the sampling distributions of magnitude statistics based on association are invariably skewed.

2.3.1 Simultaneous Confidence Intervals

The preceding formulas provide confidence intervals for a given contrast or partial epsilon squared. However, a researcher often conducts multiple contrasts, resulting in multiple confidence intervals. When we calculate 95% confidence intervals using the procedures just described, we are 95% confident that a given interval contains the true value of the population parameter. It also may be of interest to specify confidence intervals across k contrasts such that we are 95% confident that all k of the intervals contain the true population parameter, considered simultaneously. Such intervals are called *simultaneous confidence intervals*.

Procedures for calculating simultaneous confidence intervals use the same formulas as described in the preceding sections but with a different value for $t_{CRITICAL}$ or $z_{CRITICAL}$. The critical values correspond to those dictated by the statistical method for controlling experimentwise error rates. However, methods that rely on stagewise or stepwise procedures for controlling experimentwise error rates (e.g., the modified Bonferroni test) cannot be used as a basis for forming simultaneous confidence intervals. The most common approach relies on the traditional Bonferroni correction in which $t_{CRITICAL}$ or $z_{CRITICAL}$ is based on an alpha level of α (the per comparison alpha level) divided by the number of contrasts performed within the family of contrasts. For example, if there are three contrasts, then the $z_{CRITICAL}$ would be based on alpha / 3 = .05 / 3 = .0167, yielding a $z_{CRITICAL}$ of 2.39. A disadvantage of the Bonferroni method is that it is conservative, often yielding confidence intervals that are quite wide and that may lead to the interval estimation equivalent of a Type II error. Alternative approaches based on Scheffé's method and methods focused on all possible pairwise comparisons of means are discussed in Maxwell and Delaney (1990) and Toothaker (1993). We will consider these approaches in Chapter 4.

2.3.2 Criticisms of Interval Estimation Approaches

Confidence intervals, when applied to both parameter estimates and indexes of effect size, have many attractive features. They combine features of both classic hypothesis testing (because if the confidence interval does not contain the value of zero, then the null hypothesis is rejected) and magnitude estimation. They directly address the tendency for a researcher to interpret his or her parameter estimates and indexes of effect size without regard to sampling error because the size of the interval becomes smaller as sampling error decreases; a point estimate in conjunction with a large confidence interval makes clear that the analyst must be cautious when interpreting the results.

Most of the criticisms raised with respect to indexes of effect size apply with equal vigor to interval estimation approaches when the focus is on estimating confidence intervals for effect size indexes. After all, confidence intervals only augment the point estimate by specifying an interval around it so that one can appreciate the effects of sampling error. It is interesting to conjecture how a researcher might use confidence intervals in practice if the classic hypothesis-testing framework were abandoned, as several methodologists have suggested. Suppose, for example, that a researcher is evaluating an intervention designed to increase intelligence of young children and that the study uses a standard intelligence test with a mean of 100 and a standard deviation of 10. The researcher decides that a 3-point increase in intelligence scores, on average, is the minimum change that is required for the intervention to be judged worthwhile. We refer to this criterion as a *threshold value* (TV) because if the difference between population means exceeds this threshold, then the effect of the intervention is said to be "meaningful" or "significant." Actually, there are two TVs in most investigations: a negative one (to reflect the case in which the population mean difference is negative) and a positive one (to reflect the case in which the population mean difference is positive). The TVs for this study are −3.0 (whereby the intervention is judged to have a detrimental effect on intelligence) and 3.0 (whereby the intervention is judged to have a positive effect on intelligence). In general, the TVs for a study will be of equal magnitude but opposite in sign. Let us consider five different scenarios that might result in the comparison of means for the experimental and control groups.

First, suppose that the 95% confidence interval for the mean difference was 3.5 to 8.5. In this case, the conclusion is straightforward. The lower limit of the confidence interval exceeds the upper TV, so that the researcher can be reasonably confident that the program exceeds his or her TVs.

Second, suppose that the 95% confidence interval for the mean difference was 0.5 to 2.5. Although this result is statistically significant by classic hypothesis-testing methods, the researcher can be reasonably confident that the TV of 3 points in the intelligence quotient was not attained because the upper limit of the confidence interval is less than the TV of primary interest. Again, the conclusion is straightforward from an interval estimation perspective; the program was not effective.

Third, suppose that the 95% confidence interval ranged from –8.5 to –3.5. In this case, the evidence suggests not only that the program was ineffective but that it actually had a detrimental effect, because the upper limit of the confidence interval is less than the negative TV.

Fourth, suppose that the 95% confidence interval ranged from –2.0 to 4.0. In this case, the confidence interval contains the TV of 3.0, meaning that the intervention might plausibly have an effect that exceeds the positive TV or that it has an effect that is less than the positive TV. What is the investigator to conclude? The problem in this case is that the confidence interval is too large for the investigator to make any conclusions with confidence. The presence of at least one of the TVs within the interval means that one cannot confidently conclude that the program has an effect.

As a final scenario, suppose that the 95% confidence interval ranged from 2.0 to 8.0 with the sample mean difference equal to 5.0. In this case, one of the TVs is contained within the interval (3.0), indicating that the investigator should *not* conclude that the intervention was effective. But note that the sample mean was considerably larger than 3.0 and that the result was statistically significant (i.e., the null hypothesis was rejected). Classic null hypothesis testing would lead us to conclude that the intervention is effective, but the interval estimation approach suggests otherwise (e.g., the confidence interval is too wide to make such a conclusion with confidence).

Classical hypothesis testing, as traditionally applied, sets a TV of zero. If we conclude that two populations do not share the same mean, then we say that the result is statistically significant and are inclined to act on this significance in a substantive way. This is tantamount to using a TV of zero. By using a nonzero TV in interval estimation, a more stringent criterion is used to declare a result significant. As such, interval estimation approaches probably will require larger sample sizes than will traditional hypothesis-testing strategies to make unambiguous conclusions, everything else being equal. It is, of course, possible to set a TV to a nonzero value in classic hypothesis tests that use Equation 1.2. For example, instead of testing a null hypothesis that the difference between two population means is zero, the null hypothesis can be specified such that the difference between two means is equal to some nonzero value.

Many of the decisions we make on the basis of research are binary in character and require the specification of TV values when evaluated experimentally. Do we implement a new program/policy or not? Do we switch a medication or not? If asked, should a parent tell his or her adolescent son or daughter that the parent used drugs when he or she was a teenager? Researchers and policy analysts often are forced to choose one course of action over another by virtue of the binary character of the decision. We believe that if one is to adopt a magnitude estimation or interval estimation philosophy in experiments relevant to such contexts, then one must make a clear case for a particular TV (e.g., the 3.0 increase in intelligence) that will cause the researcher or policymaker to act one way or the other. This is not an easy task, and it forces the analyst to think far beyond statistical issues.

For many theory tests, we are not forced to make a binary choice. Rather, the validity of a theory can be thought of in terms of "degrees of confidence," for example, that we are 80% confident in the viability of the theory. In interval estimation approaches, the size of the interval and whether it contains the TV influence the degree of confidence we place in a theory based on an experimental outcome. Binary- versus confidence-based perspectives on the validity of a theory have enjoyed considerable discussion in the literature on Bayesian statistics and philosophy of science. Interested readers can consult Howson and Urbach (1989), Chow (1988, 1989), and Folger (1989).

In the late 1980s, an associate editor of the *American Journal of Public Health*, one of the premier journals in the field of public health, decided to ban traditional tests of statistical significance from the journal and, instead, (strongly) encouraged researchers to report confidence intervals for the analysis of population parameters (Shrout, 1997). The editorial policy was implemented through "revise-and-resubmit" letters from the editor to prospective authors, and the letters were characterized by Fleiss (1986) as having the following content:

> All references to statistical hypothesis testing and statistical significance should be removed from the paper. I ask that you delete *p* values as well as comments about statistical significance. If you do not agree with my standards (concerning the inappropriateness of significance tests), you should feel free to argue the point, or simply ignore what you consider to be my misguided view by publishing elsewhere. As editor, however, I can hardly be expected to accept papers that violate the scientific principle that I espouse. (quoted on p. 559)

This policy led to heated exchanges about the merits of such a position, with a major complaint being that researchers avoided specifying TVs and instead reported results with wide confidence intervals that would not have been published using traditional significance levels. The ban was dropped when the term of the editor ended, but the events made salient the critical nature of the issues of defining TVs and developing standards for acceptable widths of confidence intervals. We believe that researchers who conduct traditional null hypothesis tests should at least think about what they would do if they received such a revise-and-resubmit letter from an editor and the implications that adopting such a policy would have for the conclusions they ultimately make in the context of their research.

In sum, interval estimation approaches augment point estimation approaches by providing a confidence interval around the point estimate that gives the researcher an appreciation for sampling error. Interval estimation approaches often will require the careful justification of TVs for purposes of declaring an effect to be meaningful or trivial. Such justification may be difficult and the source of scientific debate. In general, an effect can be said to be nontrivial if either (a) the lower limit of the confidence interval exceeds the positive TV or (b) the upper limit of the confidence interval is less than the negative TV. Confidence intervals that contain a TV yield ambiguous conclusions.

In traditional null hypothesis testing, it often is emphasized that one can never accept the null hypothesis. Rather, we can either reject it or fail to reject it. In interval estimation approaches, the researcher can, in some senses, "accept the null." Consider the scenario in which the confidence interval for evaluating the intervention directed at raising intelligence was 0.5 to 2.5. Suppose that we conducted two directional tests using a classic null hypothesis-testing paradigm, one testing the hypothesis that the population mean difference is greater than the TV of −3.0 and the second testing the hypothesis that the population mean difference is less than the TV of 3.0. Based on the confidence interval, we know that we would reject both null hypotheses and confidently conclude that the population difference is, indeed, less than 3.0 and that it also is greater than −3.0. This is reflected by the fact that the lower limit of the confidence interval is greater than −3.0 and the upper limit is less than 3.0. If the null hypothesis is that there is no *meaningful* difference between the two population means (as defined by the TVs), then in this case we can accept the null hypothesis (with 95% confidence). Because this logic involves two one-tailed tests, some methodologists recommend using 90% confidence intervals rather than 95% confidence intervals. In general, when the lower limit of the confidence interval is greater than the negative TV and the upper limit of the confidence interval is less than the positive TV, we can conclude that there is no meaningful effect. For an alternative approach to this issue that also relies on confidence intervals, see Rosenthal and Rubin (1994).

2.3.3 Defining a Small Confidence Interval

For obvious reasons, small confidence intervals usually are more desirable than large confidence intervals, and researchers should strive to design studies to minimize interval width. What constitutes a "small enough" confidence interval? There is no simple answer to this question because it concerns how much sampling error one is willing to tolerate in one's estimates, and this can vary as a function of the substantive domain. One possibility is to apply Cohen's (1988) criteria for effect size in which a small width corresponds to a δ of $\pm.20$, a medium width to a δ of $\pm.50$, and a large width to a δ of $\pm.80$. For example, suppose that in the intervention study on intelligence, the population standard deviation of the intelligence test used as the dependent variable was 10. Extrapolating from Equation 2.1, a small interval width would be $\pm(.20)(10) = \pm2.0$, a medium interval width would be $\pm(.50)(10) = \pm5.0$, and a large interval width would be $\pm(.80)(10) = \pm8.0$.

Because a confidence interval reflects sampling error, one strategy for reducing the size of the confidence interval is to increase sample size. For contrasts that use Equation 1.2 and in which the sample size will be larger than 30, a quick, rough estimate of the sample size needed to obtain an interval of a specified width for a given contrast is

$$N_{DW} = [(z_{CRITICAL})^2(\sigma^2)(\Sigma c_j^2)] / [.25(CI_{DW})^2]$$

where N_{DW} is the approximate sample size per group necessary to achieve the desired width, $z_{CRITICAL}$ is the critical value for the specified α in a standard normal distribution, σ is a "best guess" of the pooled within-population standard deviation, Σc_j^2 is the sum of the squared contrast coefficients used in Equation 1.2, and CI_{DW} is the desired width of the confidence interval. For example, in the intervention study with intelligence that had two groups (an experimental group and a control group), the investigator may want to achieve a confidence interval within -2 and $+2$ units of the point estimate for the contrast defined by the numerator of Equation 1.2 (but with two means instead of four). Thus, $CI_{DW} = 4.0$. Based on past research, the investigator might guess that the pooled population standard deviation is 10. The contrast coefficients are $+1$ and -1 for the two means, so $\Sigma c_j^2 = 2$. This yields $[(1.96^2)(10.0^2)(2)] / [(.25)(4^2)]$, which equals 192. Thus, the sample size per group that would be needed is approximately 190 or a total sample size of 380. For additional methods for determining sample size relative to interval width, see Wilcox (1996).

3. A COMPLETE NUMERICAL EXAMPLE

In this section, we illustrate the application of all three frameworks (hypothesis testing, magnitude estimation, and interval estimation) to a 2 × 2 factorial design. The study is an all between-subjects factorial design and focuses on educational messages provided to high school students about drunk driving and alcohol use. The first factor is how the information contained in the message is framed. When discussing the consequences of alcohol use and drunk driving, one can emphasize either the positive consequences of not engaging in the behavior or the negative consequences of engaging in the behavior. Both strategies focus on the same information, but the former uses a "positive" frame of reference and the latter uses a "negative" frame of reference. The research question is which will be more effective, a positive or negative frame of reference. In this study, the researcher believes that, in general, a positive frame of reference will be more effective than a negative frame of reference because the latter will tend to raise anxiety levels and, as a defense mechanism, individuals will process the message less vigorously to avoid feeling anxious. The second factor is the source of the message. The (identical) message is attributed to either a peer who has recovered from a serious drinking problem or a health professional. The research question is whether the peer will be more influential than the adult. Based on identification theory, the researcher believes that the peer source will be more effective than the adult source because the peer source is more similar to the message recipient. Finally, the investigator believes that the effect of framing may differ depending on the source. Specifically, he or she believes that the mean difference in positive versus negative framing will be larger for the peer source than for the adult source. The prediction derives from the idea that because of increased attention to the peer source, the anxiety provoked by the negative frame will be even greater than that for the adult source, leading to a larger mean difference for the peer source.

Students were provided a two-page pamphlet to read that conformed to one of the cells of the design. One week after reading it, they were given a recall test to see how many points they could correctly recall from it. Recall scores could range from 0 to 25 with higher scores indicating better recall. The study used 30 individuals in each cell of the design for a total N of 120.

We begin with the traditional hypothesis-testing perspective. The researcher decides that the contrasts of interest correspond to the main effects and interaction effect in the context of the moderator or cell mean approach.

56

TABLE 3.1

Means and Summary Table for Example on Message Recall

Message Frame	Source		Row Mean
	Peer	Adult	
Negative	10.27	9.20	9.73
Positive	13.87	6.90	10.38
Column mean	12.07	8.05	
Grand mean = 10.06			

Source	SS	df	MS	F	p
Message frame (A)	12.67	1	12.67	0.82	< .368
Source (B)	484.01	1	484.01	31.21	< .001
A × B	261.07	1	261.07	16.84	< .001
Within	1,798.83	116	15.51		
Total	2,556.59	119			

NOTE: SS = sum of squares; MS = mean square.

Thus, the focus is on mean differences and differences between mean differences. After ensuring that the assumptions of the analysis of variance (ANOVA) are satisfied and that there are no outliers, the researcher conducts a 2 × 2 factorial ANOVA. Table 3.1 presents relevant means and the summary table for the analysis.

The main effect of message frame was not statistically significant for an alpha level of .05. This raises the possibility of a Type II error for this contrast. The researcher decides to conduct an analysis of statistical power.[9] Based on past research and clinical experience, the researcher decides that a mean difference of three or four points recalled might be critical. The researcher therefore decides to determine the statistical power for the ability to detect a mean difference of at least three items. In addition, the researcher decides to examine the statistical power for detecting small, medium, and large effect sizes as defined by Cohen (1988). Cohen defines effect sizes in terms of δ (Equation 2.1). A small effect size is when δ = .20, a medium effect size is when δ =.50, and a large effect size is when δ =.80 (see Cohen, 1988, for elaboration on the rationale for these choices). We use the square root of MS_{WITHIN} as an estimate of the population standard deviation. This equals 3.94. The power analysis is conducted using a computer program for the one-sample t test, as described earlier. The estimated statistical power to detect a mean difference of three items is greater than .98. The estimated power for a small, medium, and large effect size were .19, .77, and .99. However, the researcher is not particularly concerned with the small effect size; a δ of .20 represents a mean difference of less than one recalled item because, by manipulation of Equation 2.1, the population mean difference equals $(\delta)(\sigma)$, which we estimate is $(.20)(3.94) = .79$ for a small effect size. Thus, low statistical power is not problematic.

Next, the researcher turns to the main effect of message source. Some methodologists believe that it is not appropriate to analyze main effects in the presence of a statistical interaction. According to this perspective, a main effect should reflect a constant effect of an independent variable on a dependent variable that generalizes across all levels of the moderator variable. A statistically significant interaction suggests that no such constant effect exists. Other methodologists argue that main effects may be meaningful in the presence of an interaction. These methodologists conceptualize main effects as the *average* effect of an independent variable on a dependent variable across levels of the moderator and argue that information about such average effects may be useful. Also, some theoretical questions dictate the examination of main effects no matter what the outcome of an interaction analysis is. We pursue more detailed analyses of the main effect in deference to methodologists with such an orientation, recognizing that the practice is controversial. The mean number of points recalled for the "peer" source was 12.07 and for the "adult" source was 8.05. This yields a mean difference of 4.02 ($p < .001$). In general, the message from the peer tended to yield, on average, better recall than that from the adult.

The interaction effect is conceptualized as a contrast comparing the mean difference between positive and negative message frames for peers as opposed to adults (i.e., the source of the message is the moderator variable). The mean difference for peers was $13.87 - 10.27 = 3.60$, and the corresponding difference for adults was $6.90 - 9.20 = -2.30$. The difference between these differences $(3.60 - (-2.30) = 5.90)$ is statistically significant ($p < .05$), as indicated by the F ratio in the summary table. Thus, the effect of message framing differs as a function of the source of the message.

It is useful to supplement this analysis with simple main-effect contrasts. As noted in Chapter 1, simple main-effects analysis does *not* elucidate the nature and source of an interaction effect in a factorial design (Kirk, 1995). However, a researcher often will want to know whether there is an effect of an independent variable on a dependent variable at each level of the moderator variable, and simple main-effects analysis provides perspectives

TABLE 3.2
Contrast Coefficients for Persuasion Study

	$\bar{X}_{11}$	$\bar{X}_{12}$	$\bar{X}_{21}$	$\bar{X}_{22}$
Sample mean value	10.27	9.20	13.87	6.90
Main effect of message frame	−.50	−.50	.50	.50
Main effect of source	.50	−.50	.50	−.50
Interaction effect	−1	1	1	−1
Simple main effect of framing for peer source	−1	0	1	0
Simple main effect of framing for adult source	0	−1	0	1

on this. Thus, we can ask (a) whether there is an effect of message framing (in terms of mean differences) for just the peer source and (b) whether there is an effect of message framing (in terms of mean differences) for just the adult source. The simple main effect for the peer source uses Equation 1.2 with the contrast coefficients of $c_1 = -1$, $c_2 = 0$, $c_3 = 1$, and $c_4 = 0$ (see Table 3.2). The contrast yields a t value of 3.54, which is statistically significant ($p < .001$). The coefficients for the simple main effect for the adult source are $c_1 = 0$, $c_2 = -1$, $c_3 = 0$, and $c_4 = 1$. The resulting t is −2.26, which also is statistically significant ($p < .05$). Both of these simple main effects remain statistically significant if a modified Bonferroni control is invoked across the two contrasts.

In sum, the traditional hypothesis-testing approach yields the following conclusions. Contrary to predictions, there is no strong evidence for an overall main effect of message framing. However, there is evidence for a main effect of message source such that peers, on average, tend to be more effective than adults (as least in terms of recall of the message). The statistically significant interaction effect indicates that the effect of message framing on recall differs as a function of message source. When the message source is a peer, positive messages tend to produce, on average, more recall than do negative messages. When the message source is an adult, positive messages tend to produce, on average, less recall than do negative messages.

We now augment this with perspectives from magnitude estimation and interval estimation. Table 3.2 presents the contrast coefficients that were used in the preceding analyses, and Table 3.3 presents the relevant effect sizes and confidence intervals for each contrast. We focus first on effect sizes and confidence intervals in terms of the mean differences in raw scores (i.e., the rows labeled "parameter value," "lower 95% limit of

TABLE 3.3
Results for Magnitude Estimation and Interval Estimation

	PF-NF	Peer-Adult	Interaction	PF-NF for Peer Only	PF-NF for Adult Only
Parameter value	0.65	4.02	5.90	3.60	−2.30
Estimated standard error of parameter value	0.72	0.72	1.44	1.02	1.02
t ratio for parameter value	0.90	5.59	4.10	3.54	−2.26
p value for *t* ratio	< .37	< .001	< .001	< .001	< .026
Lower 95% limit of parameter value	−0.76	2.61	3.08	1.61	−4.29
Upper 95% limit of parameter value	2.06	5.43	8.72	5.59	−0.31
Hedge's *d*	0.16	1.01	1.49	0.91	−0.58
Partial epsilon squared	0.00	0.21	0.12	0.09	0.03
Lower 95% limit of partial proportion of explained variance	0.00	0.09	0.04	0.02	<.01
Upper 95% limit of partial proportion of explained variance	0.06	0.33	0.24	0.20	0.13

NOTE: PF = positive frame; NF = negative frame.

parameter value," and "upper 95% limit of parameter value" in Table 3.3). As noted earlier, the investigator established threshold values (TVs) equal to −3.0 and +3.0. The first contrast in Table 3.3 is the main effect of message framing. The point estimate for this main effect was 0.65, and the confidence limits were −.76 to 2.06. We can confidently conclude from these intervals that the main effect of message framing, if any, is trivial in magnitude, because the upper limit is less than the positive TV and the lower limit is larger than the negative TV.

The second contrast is the main effect of source. The point estimate for the parameter was 4.02. The 95% confidence limits were 2.61 and 5.43. The TV of 3.0 falls within this interval, so we cannot confidently conclude that the mean difference in recall as a function of source is meaningful.

The third contrast is the interaction effect, and it yielded a point estimate of 5.90 and confidence limits of 3.08 and 8.72. We can confidently conclude that the interaction effect is meaningful, because the lower limit is larger than the positive TV.

The simple main-effects analysis yielded confidence limits of 1.61 and 5.59 for the peer source and −4.29 and −0.31 for the adult source. Both of these intervals contain an instance of the TV. We cannot conclude with confidence that message framing for either source considered separately has a meaningful effect on the tendency to recall the message. This is true whether we use per comparison or simultaneous confidence intervals for the family of simple main effects. We *can* say with confidence that the two sources produce differential effects when compared to each other (as reflected by the overall interaction). But we cannot confidently characterize what is happening with each source individually (as reflected by the simple main effects).

Having analyzed the data in terms of interval estimation as applied to raw means, it seems moot to characterize the data in terms of standardized mean differences or percentage of variance accounted for. The conclusions should be the same except for differences that occur in the accuracy of the estimating equations for the respective parameters. For example, to characterize the analysis in terms of δ, one would begin by describing values for the TV but in units of δ rather than in raw score units. TVs of -3.0 and $+3.0$ raw score units translate into values of $-.76$ and $.76$ for δ (as computed by Equation 2.1 and using the square root of MS_{WITHIN} as the value of σ). But if we already have conducted the analysis in terms of -3.0 and $+3.0$ raw score units as the TVs, then why bother doing it with a δ of $.76$, which is the numerical equivalent of 3.0 raw score units but rescaled to units of δ?

One reason for doing so is that some readers of a research report feel more comfortable interpreting one type of effect size index than another. For example, some researchers might prefer to think of the parameters in terms of percentage of explained variance rather than raw mean differences, finding percentage of explained variance indexes to be more intuitively appealing. A second reason is that other scientists may not agree with the TVs suggested by an investigator and may want to make a case for alternative TVs. The scientist may find it easiest to make a case in terms of δ or percentage of variance accounted for, and the presentation of such indexes facilitates discussion in this respect.[10]

It is interesting to compare the conclusions from the interval estimation method to those from classic hypothesis testing. Consistent with our previous discussion, the interval estimation approach led to characterizations of fewer "meaningful" effects than did the traditional hypothesis-testing framework that relies on strict statistical significance. This is because the two approaches use different TVs, with the traditional hypothesis-testing framework using less stringent TVs than the interval estimation framework.[11] Again, we emphasize the importance of having carefully justified TVs.

4. DESIGNS WITH MORE THAN TWO LEVELS AND HIGHER ORDER DESIGNS

The previous chapters focused on 2×2 factorial designs. The concepts developed for 2×2 designs form the foundation for analysis and interpretation of more complex factorial designs. In this chapter, we first consider factorial designs that have more than two levels per factor. We then consider factorial designs consisting of three or more factors.

4.1 A 3×2 Factorial Design

To illustrate the analysis of factorial designs involving more than two levels, we use a 3×2 between-subjects factorial design in which an investigator asked individuals the number of children that they want to have in their completed families. The researcher wanted to assess the impact of religion (Catholic vs. Protestant vs. Jewish) and religiosity (religious vs. not religious) on desired family size. The cell mean or moderator approach was most consistent with the questions that the researcher wanted to address; hence, we adopt this orientation. A total of 50 women from each cell of the design were interviewed. The relevant means and summary table for the analysis are presented in Table 4.1.

Both of the main effects were statistically significant, as was the interaction effect. Suppose that for theoretical reasons, the researcher was interested in comparing the main-effect means for religion collapsing across religiosity. Because the main effect of religion has three levels, multiple comparison procedures need to be applied to isolate the main-effect mean differences that are of theoretical interest. One possibility would be to apply the logic of Equation 1.2 (but with six means instead of four), define the c values that isolate the main-effect contrasts of interest (assuming that they are single degree of freedom contrasts), and then apply the modified Bonferroni method to control for the experimentwise error rate within the family of contrasts focused on the main effect. Rows 2 to 4 of Table 4.2 present the contrast coefficients that specify all possible pairwise contrasts for the main-effect means for religion. The magnitude estimation and interval estimation perspectives described in Chapters 1 and 2 also can be applied to each of these contrasts. If low statistical power is a concern for any of these contrasts, then multiple comparison methods exist that yield greater levels of statistical power than the modified Bonferroni method, and these alternatives should be pursued accordingly. The

TABLE 4.1
Means and Summary Table for Desired Number of Children Example

	Religious	Not Religious	Row Mean
Catholic	3.80	2.10	2.95
Protestant	3.10	2.02	2.56
Jew	1.98	1.96	1.97
Column mean	2.96	2.03	
Grand mean = 2.49			

Source	SS	df	MS	F	p
Religion (A)	48.69	2	24.34	26.62	< .001
Religiosity (B)	65.33	1	65.33	71.44	< .001
A × B	36.09	2	18.04	19.73	< .001
Within	268.88	294	0.91		
Total	418.99	299			

NOTE: SS = sum of squares; MS = mean square.

issue of choosing an appropriate multiple comparison method for a main-effect analysis is beyond the scope of this monograph, and interested readers are referred to the excellent discussions by Kirk (1995) and Toothaker (1993). Our focus is on explicating methods for elucidating moderated relationships, so we turn to the analysis of the two-way interaction.

As noted in Chapter 1, the moderator approach requires that we specify a moderator variable and a *focal* independent variable whose effect on the dependent variable is said to be moderated by the moderator variable. We use religiosity as the focal independent variable and religion as the moderator variable. The 3 × 2 design actually consists of three 2 × 2 subtables that result from combining all possible pairs of levels of one factor with all possible pairs of levels of the other factor:

	C	J
R	3.80	1.98
NR	2.10	1.96

	P	J
R	3.10	1.98
NR	2.02	1.96

	C	P
R	3.80	3.10
NR	2.10	2.02

$(3.80 - 2.10) - (1.98 - 1.96)$
$= 1.68$

$(3.10 - 2.02) - (1.98 - 1.96)$
$= 1.06$

$(3.80 - 2.10) - (3.10 - 2.02)$
$= 0.62$

TABLE 4.2
Contrasts for Analysis of Desired Number of Children

	$\overline{X}_{11}$	$\overline{X}_{12}$	$\overline{X}_{21}$	$\overline{X}_{22}$	$\overline{X}_{31}$	$\overline{X}_{32}$
Sample mean value	3.80	2.10	3.10	2.02	1.98	1.96
Main-effect contrast: C versus J	.50	.50	0	0	−.50	−.50
Main-effect contrast: P versus J	0	0	.50	.50	−.50	−.50
Main-effect contrast: C versus P	.50	.50	−.50	−.50	0	0
Interaction contrast: (R, NR) × (C, J)	1	−1	0	0	−1	1
Interaction contrast: (R, NR) × (P, J)	0	0	1	−1	−1	1
Interaction contrast: (R, NR) × (C, P)	1	−1	−1	1	0	0
Simple main effect: Religiosity for Catholics	1	−1	0	0	0	0
Simple main effect: Religiosity for Protestants	0	0	1	−1	0	0
Simple main effect: Religiosity for Jews	0	0	0	0	1	−1

NOTE: C = Catholic; J = Jew; P = Protestant; R = religious; NR = not religious.

where C = Catholic, P = Protestant, J = Jewish, R = religious, and NR = not religious. We refer to such 2 × 2 subtables as pairwise 2 × 2 subtables to distinguish them from other 2 × 2 subtables that will be discussed later. A parameter value corresponding to an interaction effect (the difference between mean differences) is calculated for each subtable and appears directly below the corresponding subtable. Consider the parameter value for the first subtable, 1.68. This parameter reflects the difference between religious and nonreligious Catholics minus the difference between religious and nonreligious Jews. The fact that it is nonzero (1.68) suggests that this 2 × 2 interaction contrast is contributing to the overall interaction effect that was observed between religion and religiosity. However, it is possible that the nonzero value merely reflects sampling error, so we want to conduct a formal statistical test of this interaction contrast. This is accomplished using the logic of Equation 1.2, but applied to the six group means. The fifth row of Table 4.2 presents the relevant contrast coefficients, and Table 4.3 presents the results of the analysis. It can be seen that the difference between mean differences for this contrast was statistically significant ($p < .05$). Similar analyses are performed for the other 2 × 2 subtables, and these also are statistically significant, even when a modified Bonferroni test is applied across the contrasts (see Tables 4.2 and 4.3). Inspection of the cell means in conjunction with these statistical tests allows us to conclude that (a) the effects of religiosity on the number of

TABLE 4.3

Results for Interaction Contrasts and
Simple Main Effects for Desired Family Size Example

	IC_1	IC_2	IC_3	SME_1	SME_2	SME_3
Parameter value	1.68	1.06	0.62	1.70	1.08	0.02
Estimated standard error of parameter value	0.27	0.27	0.27	0.19	0.19	0.19
t ratio for parameter value	6.23	3.93	2.30	8.91	5.66	0.10
p value for t ratio	< .001	< .001	.02	< .001	< .001	.92
Lower 95% limit of parameter value	1.15	0.53	0.09	1.33	0.71	–0.35
Upper 95% limit of parameter value	2.21	1.59	1.15	2.07	1.45	0.39
Hedge's d	1.76	1.11	0.65	1.78	1.13	0.02
Partial epsilon squared	.11	.05	.01	.21	.10	.00
Lower 95% limit of partial proportion of explained variance	.06	.01	.001	.14	.04	.00
Upper 95% limit of partial proportion of explained variance	.19	.10	.056	.29	.17	.01

NOTE: IC_1 = interaction contrast for (Religious, Not Religious) × (Catholic, Jew); IC_2 = interaction contrast for (Religious, Not Religious) × (Protestant, Jew); IC_3 = interaction contrast for (Religious, Not Religious) × (Catholic, Protestant); SME_1 = simple main effect of religiosity for Catholics; SME_2 = simple main effect of religiosity for Protestants; SME_3 = simple main effect of religiosity for Jews.

desired children are more pronounced for Catholics than for Jews, (b) the effects of religiosity on the number of desired children are more pronounced for Catholics than for Protestants, and (c) the effects of religiosity on the number of desired children are more pronounced for Protestants than for Jews.

Another set of contrasts that may be of theoretical interest is the simple main effects of religiosity at each level of religion. These contrasts tell us whether there is a statistically significant difference in the dependent variable as a function of the focal independent variable at each level of the moderator variable. The contrast coefficients for the three simple main effects are presented in Table 4.2, and the results are presented in Table 4.3. The simple main effects for religiosity at the levels of Catholic and Protestant both were statistically significant, but this was not true for Jews. This pattern of results maintained when the modified Bonferroni procedure was applied to control the experimentwise error rate across the three contrasts. Thus, religious individuals tend to prefer more children, on average, than do nonreligious individuals in the case of Catholics and Protestants. Because the religious/not-religious differential was not statistically significant for Jews, the issue of a Type II error is relevant. The investigator defined a small effect size as one fifth of a child (i.e., a mean of 0.20 on the dependent variable) and, using the power analysis strategy from Chapter 1, finds approximate power of 0.18 for this contrast. Thus, low statistical power is problematic. We leave it as an exercise for readers to apply the magnitude estimation and interval estimation perspectives to the data using the results in Table 4.3.

We can summarize the steps we used for analyzing an interaction effect with more than one degree of freedom as follows:

Step 1: Specify all 2 × 2 subtables that are of theoretical interest. For exploratory research, this typically will be all possible pairwise 2 × 2 subtables. Calculate the parameter value for the two-way interaction for each subtable.

Step 2: Conduct interaction contrasts that test the significance of the parameter value for each of the tables identified in Step 1.

Step 3: Conduct any simple main-effects analyses that are of theoretical interest on the subtables identified in Step 1. The simple main-effects tests often are conducted examining the effects of the focal independent variable at each level of the moderator variable within the 2 × 2 subtables.

When executing these steps, decide whether it is appropriate to invoke controls for experimentwise error rates and, if so, specify how the different families of contrasts should be defined and what method of control will be used. We discuss this issue in more depth shortly.

The three-step approach just described should be viewed as a guideline, not a rule. There will be occasions where the theoretical questions dictate a different set of contrasts, but the three-step strategy will have widespread applicability. Our strategy differs from those suggested by many textbooks. For example, a commonly suggested approach involves the following sequence. First, test the statistical significance of the overall interaction. Second, if it is statistically significant, then conduct interaction contrasts that shed light on the sources that contribute to the overall interaction effect. Third, conduct simple main-effects analyses examining the effects of Factor A at each level of Factor B and the effects of Factor B at each level of Factor A. If the focal independent variable in a given simple-effect analysis has more than two levels, then first conduct the equivalent of a one-way analysis of variance (ANOVA) on the dependent variable as a function of the focal independent variable using the mean square error from the overall analysis as the error term. If this yields a statistically significant F ratio, then conduct follow-up tests on the one-way analysis (e.g., all possible pairwise comparisons) with an appropriate control for experimentwise error rates (e.g., a Tukey HSD test). We comment on each of these recommendations relative to our approach.

4.1.1 Testing the Omnibus Interaction

The approach we advocate does not require that the overall omnibus interaction effect be statistically significant for purposes of pursuing interaction contrasts. This is because the most commonly used controls for experimentwise error rates (e.g., the modified Bonferroni test, the Scheffé method) do not require that the omnibus test be used as a "screen" to effectively control experimentwise error rates. Indeed, studies suggest that using the omnibus test as a screen lessens the statistical power of these multiple comparison procedures (Bernhardson, 1975). There are some two-step multiple comparison procedures that require a statistically significant omnibus test, but most of these are not widely recommended. The bottom line is that if one applies a method for controlling experimentwise error rates that does not require an omnibus test as a screen, then one can move directly to the contrasts of interest. For a more detailed discussion of these issues, see Bernhardson (1975), Kirk (1995), and Toothaker (1993).

Although the omnibus F test for interaction effects with $df > 1$ is not essential, a researcher can use the test as an effort-saving device. For example, if the omnibus interaction effect is not even remotely close to being statistically significant in an exploratory study using a 3×3 factorial design, then the researcher may choose not to pursue the many contrasts underlying the interaction because they are almost certain to be trivial and statistically nonsignificant.

Another reason that a researcher might wish to evaluate an omnibus interaction effect is if he or she is interested in documenting the effect size of the overall effect using an index such as partial eta squared. For example, one might want to estimate the overall proportion of explained variance that the Religion × Religiosity interaction effect accounts for relative to the total variability (instead of focusing only on the effect sizes of separate single degree of freedom contrasts that are part of the interaction). Equation 2.6 can be used for this purpose with confidence intervals being estimated using Fowler's approach, as described earlier.

4.1.2 Conducting Interaction Contrasts

One of the most useful pieces of information for exploring an omnibus interaction is the 2×2 subtable. More often than not, decomposition strategies lead the researcher to focus on one or more 2×2 subtables. This is why we developed in-depth the analysis of 2×2 designs in Chapter 1. If a subtable is larger than 2×2 (e.g., 3×2), then a statistically significant interaction contrast on that subtable leaves open the question of whether one or more of the 2×2 interactions contained within it are trivial in size. Our general philosophy is to move directly to those 2×2 contrasts that are of theoretical significance and conduct a thorough analysis of each 2×2 subtable using the procedures described in Chapter 1 (with appropriate controls for experimentwise error rates). This approach is meaningful when using the moderator conceptualization of interaction effects. When a treatment effect conceptualization is pursued, the focus is not on 2×2 subtables but rather on the interaction treatment effects associated with a given cell of the design.

The strategy illustrated with our example evaluated all pairwise 2×2 subtables, and this is typical of exploratory research. One problem with such a strategy is that the number of 2×2 subtables becomes quite large for designs with many levels of each independent variable, thereby increasing the experimentwise error rate. For example, in a 4×2 design there are 6 pairwise 2×2 subtables, in a 3×3 design there are 9 pairwise 2×2 subtables, and in a 4×4 design there are 36 pairwise 2×2 subtables. Although procedures can be invoked to control the experimentwise error rate across these interaction contrasts, statistical power quickly becomes an issue when such controls are applied to so many contrasts. There are several strategies that can be used to address this problem.

First, sometimes the theoretical questions are such that we need not focus on all pairwise 2×2 subtables. Rather, the theory guides us to focus on two or three 2×2 subtables. Theories also may dictate contrasts that represent linear or nonlinear trends for quantitative independent variables, which also can reduce the number of contrasts pursued (see Kirk, 1995, for discussions of trend analysis). Some methodologists prefer not to analyze all pairwise 2×2 subtables but to instead focus on 2×2 subtables that are defined in such a way that the interaction contrasts are orthogonal to one another. This strategy makes sense when the theoretical questions of interest map onto orthogonal contrasts, which rarely is the case. For descriptions of orthogonal interaction contrast strategies, see Keppel (1991) and Kirk (1995).

Another strategy that sometimes is used for designs with many levels is to conduct initial decomposition tests on subtables that are larger than 2 × 2. For example, in a 3 × 3 design, there are three possible 3 × 2 subtables, and tests for a statistically significant interaction might be performed on each of these subtables. If a given 3 × 2 interaction is statistically significant, then the three possible 2 × 2 subtables within it are explored. If not, the 2 × 2 subtables subsumed within the 3 × 2 subtable are not evaluated. When using this strategy, appropriate controls should be invoked for within-family experimentwise error rates based on a well-reasoned definition of families that takes into account the need to accommodate both Type I and Type II errors. See Boik (1993) for an elaboration of issues relevant to this strategy. Again, our preference is to move directly to the 2 × 2 tables that are of substantive interest.

A complex issue for interaction contrasts is the choice of an appropriate method for purposes of controlling experimentwise error rates. It is impossible to recommend one approach because the choice often is dependent on diverse design features. Interested readers are referred to Boik (1993), Kirk (1995), and Toothaker (1993). One general method is the modified Bonferroni approach presented in Chapter 1. A second general method is the Scheffé method. This approach compares the t^2 for a given contrast comprising a 2 × 2 subtable (which is calculated using the logic of Equation 1.2) against a critical F value that equals the $F_{CRITICAL}$ that was used for testing the omnibus interaction effect multiplied by $(k - 1)(m - 1)$, where k is the number of levels of the first factor and m is the number of levels of the second factor. For example, in the study on the desired number of children, the critical F value for the overall omnibus test, $\alpha = .05$, was 3.02. Each 2 × 2 contrast is evaluated against an F of $(3.02)(3 - 1)(2 - 1) = 6.04$. The square root of this is 2.46, which can then be compared directly to the t value for a given contrast.[12] The Scheffé method is generally conservative and often will have less power than the modified Bonferroni method. Other approaches to controlling experimentwise error rates for interaction contrasts are described by Boik (1993); Gabriel, Putter, and Wax (1973); and Kirk (1995).

Keppel (1991) recommends that a researcher evaluate the statistical significance of an effect first with respect to the per comparison alpha level (traditionally .05) and then a second time using the more stringent experimentwise controls. If the result is either statistically nonsignificant in both cases or statistically significant in both cases, then the conclusion is straightforward. If the results of the two comparisons are different, then the researcher may decide to suspend judgment.

4.1.3 Simple Main-Effects Analysis

As noted earlier, simple main-effects analysis is not a method for elucidating interaction effects but rather is used to address the commonly asked question of whether an independent variable has an impact on a dependent variable at a given level of the moderator variable. Whereas some textbooks recommend conducting simple main effects for Factor A at each level of Factor B and vice versa, we recommend examining only the effects of the focal independent variable at each level of the moderator variable (unless the theoretical questions dictate otherwise). Our experience has been that researchers typically frame interaction effects on a conceptual level using a moderator mentality and that applying the simple main-effect test at each level of the moderator is consistent with this orientation. The advantage of this approach is that it reduces the number of contrasts being performed, thereby lessening the probability of a Type I error across the set of contrasts.

In general, we recommend conducting the simple main-effects analysis within each of the 2×2 subtables that are of theoretical interest. If all possible pairwise 2×2 subtables are analyzed, then this strategy results in all possible pairwise comparisons of means for the focal independent variable at a given level of the moderator variable. Some researchers define a family of contrasts as *all* of the simple main effects performed and then invoke an experimentwise control procedure across these contrasts. For example, in the desired family size example, a total of three simple main effects were performed and the modified Bonferroni procedure was applied across these three contrasts.

Other researchers define the families differently. For example, some researchers argue that each level of the moderator variable defines a different family of contrasts (e.g., all possible pairwise comparisons within the first level of the moderator variable constitute one family, all possible pairwise comparisons within the second level of the moderator variable constitute a second family). Thus, one would apply the modified Bonferroni control within each of these separate families of simple main effects. Toothaker (1993) describes an approach for controlling both experimentwise and familywise error rates using the more traditional pairwise comparison procedures that rely on studentized range values (e.g., the Tukey HSD test). In general, his approach has more statistical power than does the modified Bonferroni method, and it better controls familywise error rates.

The approach described by Toothaker (1993) is based on Cicchetti (1972) and involves first specifying the total number of simple main-effect contrasts that are to be performed, C. In the desired family size example, $C = 3$. One then solves the following equation for J to the nearest whole number: $2C = J(J - 1)$. For the desired family size example, $J = 3$. J is used as the "number of means" parameter for selecting a studentized range value for purposes of applying the pairwise multiple comparison procedure of choice within each simple main-effect level. For example, if we were to apply the Tukey HSD method to the three simple main-effect analyses, then $t_{CRITICAL}$ for each test would be $q / \sqrt{2} = 3.31 / 1.41 = 2.35$, ωηερε q is the value obtained for $J = 3$ and $df_{ERROR} = 294$ from a table of studentized range values.[13] See Toothaker (1993) for the logic of the approach.

Because the modified Bonferroni procedure is easy to enact in conjunction with standard computer output, we usually apply it first to our data across all simple main-effects tests within a family. If a contrast is statistically significant with this approach, then it also will be statistically significant with methods that have more statistical power. If a contrast is not statistically significant using the modified Bonferroni approach, then we determine whether this also would be true using the traditional per comparison α of .05. If so, then the contrast also would be nonsignificant when any of the methods to control experimentwise error rates is applied. If the contrast is not statistically significant using the modified Bonferroni method but is statistically significant using the per comparison α of .05, then we pursue a more powerful procedure such as the Tukey HSD test. See Kirk (1995) and Toothaker (1993) for descriptions of these methods; see the discussion in Keselman (1994) for within-subject designs.

4.1.4 Additional Contrasts

Although our analytic strategy focused on all possible pairwise 2×2 subtables, there are other 2×2 subtables in larger factorial designs that may be of theoretical interest and that can be tested using a single degree of freedom contrast that follows from Equation 1.2. For example, in the desired family size study, a researcher might examine the effects of religiosity on desired family size as a function of whether the individual is a Christian (Catholic or Protestant) or non-Christian (Jewish). In this case, one would form the following 2×2 subtable (assuming equal cell sample sizes):

	Christian	Non-Christian
Religious	$(\overline{X}_{11} + \overline{X}_{21}) / 2$	$\overline{X}_{31}$
Not religious	$(\overline{X}_{12} + \overline{X}_{22}) / 2$	$\overline{X}_{32}$

In this table, the Christian groups represent the average of Catholics and Protestants combined, and the non-Christian groups are represented by Jews. The contrast coefficients for defining the interaction effect in this subtable in terms of differences between mean differences are $c_1 = .5$, $c_2 = -.5$, $c_3 = .5$, $c_4 = -.5$, $c_5 = -1$, and $c_6 = 1$ (using the six original cell means from the overall 3×2 design in the order presented in Table 4.2). These coefficients compare $[(\overline{X}_{11} + \overline{X}_{21}) / 2 - (\overline{X}_{12} + \overline{X}_{22}) / 2] - (\overline{X}_{31} - \overline{X}_{32})$. The contrast coefficients for examining the simple main effect of religiosity for Christians are $c_1 = .5$, $c_2 = -.5$, $c_3 = .5$, $c_4 = -.5$, $c_5 = 0$, and $c_6 = 0$. These coefficients compare $[(\overline{X}_{11} + \overline{X}_{21}) / 2] - [(\overline{X}_{12} + \overline{X}_{22}) / 2]$.

In general, there are a variety of single degree of freedom contrasts in which a researcher may be interested, and it is important that one not be constrained by the logic of the exploratory strategy that we have described or even by the mentality of moderator variables and focal independent variables. These are heuristics that help one think about interaction effects. In the end, one must identify contrasts that are of theoretical and substantive interest and pursue the analysis of those contrasts accordingly.

4.1.5 Variance Partitioning

The approach to interaction analysis described heretofore emphasizes the role of planned comparisons in which theoretically interesting single degree of freedom interaction contrasts are pursued. In the case of exploratory research, these contrasts often take the form of planned comparisons for all possible pairwise 2×2 subtables. There are other orientations to interaction analysis that should be mentioned. One approach adopts a variance partitioning philosophy in which one first identifies an overall interaction effect and then proceeds to partition the variance associated with that interaction into nonredundant sources defined by a set of orthogonal interaction contrasts. The focus of this approach is on understanding contrasts that contribute independently to the overall interaction effect, thereby partitioning the overall interaction variance into component parts. This approach also uses the contrast formula characterized by Equation 1.2 but defines multiple contrasts that are nonredundant. The number of nonredundant contrasts will equal the degrees of freedom associated with the overall interaction effect, and the sum of the eta squares for each contrast (relative to the total variability) will sum to the eta square for the overall interaction effect. A shortcoming of this approach is that the orthogonal contrasts may not correspond to contrasts that are of theoretical interest.

The strategy we propose, on the other hand, can result in situations where the contrasts have statistical redundancy. In such cases, the eta squares for the individual contrasts (relative to the total variability) may sum to a value greater than the eta square for the overall interaction effect. Although somewhat inelegant, this is not problematic so long as the researcher keeps in mind the nonredundant nature of the contrasts and so long as experimentwise error rates are controlled using methods that can accommodate such redundancy (e.g., the modified Bonferroni method). For a more detailed discussion of orthogonal contrasts, redundant contrasts, and variance partitioning, see Kirk (1995).

4.2 A $2 \times 2 \times 2$ Factorial Design

Consider an experiment in which an investigator is examining social facilitation effects, that is, the effect of having an observer present as one works on a problem. Past studies have shown that having an observer present tends to facilitate performance on simple tasks but inhibit performance on complex tasks. In this study, the researcher manipulated (a) whether an observer was present or absent while the individual worked on a task, (b) the complexity of the task (simple vs. complex), and (c) the importance of doing well on the task (by providing either no incentive or a $30 incentive for completing the task in a timely fashion). The dependent variable was the number of seconds it took to successfully complete the task. In the interest of space, we will not describe details of the study or develop the theoretical rationale for the researcher's predictions. We only note that the nature of the theory was such that the researcher was interested primarily in the three-way interaction effect and that the theoretical questions dictated conceptualizing the interaction in terms of differences between mean differences.

The means for each cell of the design are presented in Table 4.4 in conjunction with the traditional ANOVA summary table. We use these data

TABLE 4.4
Means and Summary Table for Problem-Solving Study

| | Not Important | | Important | |
	Simple	Complex	Simple	Complex
Observer absent	27.35	36.75	29.90	42.55
Observer present	31.40	57.30	30.35	76.25

Source	SS	df	MS	F	p
Observer (A)	8,628.91	1	8,628.91	74.27	< .001
Complexity (B)	22,019.56	1	22,019.56	189.52	< .001
Importance (C)	1,722.66	1	1,722.66	14.83	< .001
A × B	6,187.66	1	6,187.66	53.26	< .001
A × C	228.01	1	228.01	1.96	< .163
B × C	1,351.41	1	1,351.41	11.63	< .001
A × B × C	701.41	1	701.41	6.04	< .015
Within	17,660.35	152	116.19		
Total	58,499.94	159			

NOTE: SS = Sum of squares; MS = mean square.

to discuss the interpretation of three-way interactions and, for the moment, ignore the fact that there is sampling error in the means.

Recall that in a two-way interaction, the moderator approach to interaction analysis requires that we first specify a moderator variable that is said to moderate the impact of an independent variable on the dependent variable. For example, for the Task Complexity × Observer interaction, the investigator might specify Task Complexity as the moderator variable with the idea being that the effect of Observer on performance depends on whether the task is simple or complex. In a higher order design involving a three-way interaction, we refer to Observer as the focal independent variable and Task Complexity as a *first-order* moderator because it directly moderates the impact of the focal independent variable on the dependent variable. However, we also specify a *second-order* moderator variable. A second-order moderator variable moderates the impact of the first-order moderator on the relationship between the focal independent variable and the dependent variable. Consider the case in which Task Importance is the second-order moderator. We can specify two pairwise 2 × 2 subtables involving the first-order moderator and the focal independent variable:

Subtable 1 (low importance)		
	Simple	Complex
Absent	27.35	36.75
Present	31.40	57.30

$(27.35 - 31.40) - (36.75 - 57.30) = 16.50$

Subtable 2 (high importance)		
	Simple	Complex
Absent	29.90	42.55
Present	30.35	76.25

$(29.90 - 30.35) - (42.55 - 76.25) = 33.25$

In the first subtable, the two-way interaction is characterized by the difference between mean differences as a function of the first-order moderator variable, and the interaction parameter estimate (which appears directly beneath the subtable) is 16.50. This is the sample parameter value for the two-way interaction at the first level of the second-order moderator. The same calculations characterize the two-way interaction for the second subtable, 33.25. This is the sample parameter value for the two-way interaction at the second level of the second-order moderator. If the two-way interactions are identical for both levels of the second-order moderator, then the difference between the two two-way interaction parameter values should be zero. But in this case, the difference is nonzero (i.e., $16.50 - 33.25 = -16.75$), suggesting that a three-way interaction effect exists. These data represent samples, and it is possible that the three-way interaction parameter value in the population is zero and that the observed nonzero result of -16.75 is due to sampling error. The F ratio for the three-way interaction tests the viability of such an interpretation. A statistically significant effect indicates that the probability that the obtained result would occur if the null hypothesis of a zero three-way interaction parameter value is true is highly unlikely.

The entire three-way ANOVA can be conducted using Equation 1.2, as applied to the eight means comprising the factorial design. Although our interest is in the three-way interaction, for pedagogical purposes we present the contrast coefficients for each main effect and each interaction in the second through eighth rows of Table 4.5. We characterize the interaction analysis first in terms of classic null hypothesis testing. Relevant results are in Table 4.6.

The three-way interaction was statistically significant, $F(1, 152) = 6.04$, $p < .015$, with a parameter estimate of -16.75. To gain additional insights into the data, it often is useful to examine additional contrasts. Using an

TABLE 4.5
Contrast Coefficients for $2 \times 2 \times 2$ Factorial Design

	$\overline{X}_{111}$	$\overline{X}_{112}$	$\overline{X}_{121}$	$\overline{X}_{122}$	$\overline{X}_{211}$	$\overline{X}_{212}$	$\overline{X}_{221}$	$\overline{X}_{222}$
Sample mean value	27.35	29.90	36.75	42.55	31.40	30.35	57.30	76.25
Main effect of A	.25	.25	.25	.25	−.25	−.25	−.25	−.25
Main effect of B	.25	.25	−.25	−.25	.25	.25	−.25	−.25
Main effect of C	.25	−.25	.25	−.25	.25	−.25	.25	−.25
A × B	.50	.50	−.50	−.50	−.50	−.50	.50	.50
A × C	.50	−.50	.50	−.50	−.50	.50	−.50	.50
B × C	.50	−.50	−.50	.50	.50	−.50	−.50	.50
A × B × C	1	−1	−1	1	−1	1	1	−1
Simple effect AB at C_1	1	0	−1	0	−1	0	1	0
Simple effect AB at C_2	0	1	0	−1	0	−1	0	1
Simple effect A at B_1C_1	1	0	0	0	−1	0	0	0
Simple effect A at B_1C_2	0	1	0	0	0	−1	0	0
Simple effect A at B_2C_1	0	0	1	0	0	0	−1	0
Simple effect A at B_2C_2	0	0	0	1	0	0	0	−1

analogy from simple main-effects analysis, it may be of interest to determine whether the two-way interaction is statistically significant at each level of the second-order moderator variable. Such contrasts are called *simple interaction effects*. In the present example, there are two levels of the second-order moderator variable; hence, we conduct two simple interaction effect contrasts. The coefficients for these contrasts are provided in the 9th and 10th rows of Table 4.5. Table 4.6 presents the results for the contrasts. Both of the two-way interactions were statistically significant at each level of task importance. The difference between mean differences was 16.50 when task importance was low, $t(152) = 3.42$, $p < .001$, and it was 33.25 when task importance was high, $t(152) = 6.90$, $p < .001$. Each of these contrasts remained statistically significant when a modified Bonferroni correction for experimentwise error was introduced within the family of simple interaction effects. Thus, we can state that a statistically significant two-way interaction is operating at both levels of task importance but that it is stronger for high-importance tasks than for low-importance tasks (because the three-way interaction is significant).

Another set of contrasts that might be of interest is whether the focal independent variable has an effect on the dependent variable at each of the four levels defined by the factorial combination of the first-order moderator variable and the second-order moderator variable. These are called *simple-*

TABLE 4.6
Result for Analysis of Three-Way Interaction

	TW	SIE$_1$	SIE$_2$	SSME$_1$	SSME$_2$	SSME$_3$	SSME$_4$
Parameter value	−16.75	16.50	33.25	−4.05	−0.45	−20.55	−33.70
Estimated standard error of parameter value	6.82	4.82	4.82	3.41	3.41	3.41	3.41
t ratio for parameter value	2.46	3.42	6.90	−1.19	−0.13	−6.03	−9.89
p value for t ratio	< .015	< .001	< .001	< .237	< .895	< .001	< .001
Lower 95% limit of parameter value	−30.11	7.05	23.80	−10.73	−7.13	−27.23	−40.38
Upper 95% limit of parameter value	−3.39	25.95	42.70	2.63	6.23	−13.87	−27.02
Hedge's d	−1.55	1.52	3.07	−0.37	−0.04	−1.90	−3.11
Partial epsilon squared	.03	.07	.23	.003	.00	.19	.38
Lower 95% limit of population partial proportion of explained variance	.001	.01	.13	.000	.00	.09	.27
Upper 95% limit of population partial proportion of explained variance	.11	.16	.34	.057	.02	.30	.48

NOTE: TW = three-way interaction; SIE$_1$ = simple interaction effect for Observer × Task Complexity when task importance is low; SIE$_2$ = simple interaction effect for Observer × Task Complexity when task importance is high; SSME$_1$ = simple-simple main effect for Observer at the levels of simple task, low task importance; SSME$_2$ = simple-simple main effect for Observer at the levels of simple task, high task importance; SSME$_3$ = simple-simple main effect for Observer at the levels of complex task, low task importance; SSME$_4$ = simple-simple main effect for Observer at the levels of complex task, high task importance.

simple main effects because we evaluate the impact of the focal independent variable after fixing the levels of two factors, not one. The 11th through 14th rows of Table 4.5 present the relevant contrast coefficients, and the results are in Table 4.6. Only two of the four simple-simple main effects were statistically significant, and these indicated that there was a statistically significant effect of the presence or absence of an observer on performance when tasks were complex at both low and high task importance. These effects remained statistically significant when a modified Bonferroni correction for experimentwise error rates was applied within the family of simple-simple main effects.

The two statistically nonsignificant simple-simple main effects raise the possibility of a Type II error. Suppose that the researcher adopted Cohen's

(1988) criteria, specifying that an effect size of $\delta = .20$ was the minimal effect size that he or she wanted to be sure to detect. The best guess of the pooled population standard deviation is the square root of the mean square error, which equals 10.78. A δ of .20 translates into $(.20)(10.78) = 2.16$ seconds using the raw metric of the dependent variable. The approximate statistical power for a test of a simple-simple main effect for $\alpha = .05$, two-tailed test, $df = 152$ is .09. This is low. For a medium effect size ($\delta = .50$), the statistical power is approximately .34.

In sum, the results of the study suggest that the presence of an observer has a detrimental effect on task performance for complex tasks and that, when compared to observer effects for simple tasks, the effect is more pronounced for tasks that are high in importance than for those that are low in importance.

For the application of magnitude and interval estimation approaches, the threshold values (TVs) are -2.16 and $+2.16$, as already defined. All of the statistically significant effects described were deemed nontrivial when the logic of interval estimation was applied. The two statistically nonsignificant simple-simple main effects yielded confidence limits that included the TV value.

We can summarize the formal steps for exploring a three-way interaction with two levels per factor using the moderator approach as follows:

Step 1: Specify the focal independent variable, the first-order moderator variable, and the second-order moderator variable.

Step 2: Define the two-way interaction between the first-order moderator variable and the focal independent variable at each level of the second-order moderator variable. Calculate the parameter value for each of these two-way interactions. Compute the difference between these parameter values as a function of the second-order moderator variable. This is the parameter value for the three-way interaction. If the three-way interaction is significant, then it can be concluded that the parameter value for the three-way interaction in the population is not zero.

Step 3: For each of the two-way interactions specified in Step 2, test those simple interaction effects that are of theoretical interest.

Step 4: Specify simple-simple main effects that represent the impact of the focal independent variable on the dependent variable at the various combinations of the first- and second-order moderators. Test any simple-simple main effects that are of theoretical interest.

As before, decisions must be made about controls for experimentwise error rates and how the different families of contrasts will be defined.

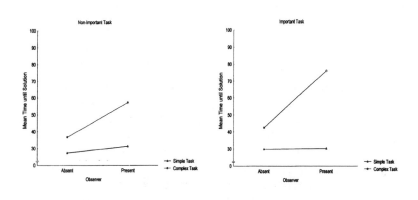

Figure 4.1.   Example of Side-by-Side Plot

For three-way designs in which factors have more than two levels, the three-way interaction is decomposed by identifying theoretically relevant 2×2 subtables and then performing formal tests of the differences in interaction parameter values between the 2×2 subtables. Simple interaction effects and simple-simple main effects also can be pursued in the context of the 2×2 subtables. Again, the primary focus is on theoretically meaningful single degree of freedom contrasts.

4.3   Four-Factor Designs

A four-factor design incorporates the same basic logic as in the preceding, but the researcher specifies a first-order moderator variable, a second-order moderator variable, and a third-order moderator variable that moderates the impact of the second-order moderator on the first-order moderator's impact on the relationship between the focal independent variable and the dependent variable. In the case of a $2 \times 2 \times 2 \times 2$ design, the four-way interaction is reflected in the difference between the parameter value for a three-way interaction at the first level of the third-order moderator variable and the parameter value for the corresponding three-way interaction at the second level of the third-order moderator variable. A four-way interaction can be explored using simple interaction effects, simple-simple interaction effects, and simple-simple-simple main effects. All of the concepts developed earlier readily apply to the four-factor case and other higher order designs.

4.4 Graphical Presentations

The graphical presentation of two-factor designs with more than two levels per factor follows the same guidelines as those discussed in Chapter 1. For three-factor designs, the most common graphical strategy is to form side-by-side plots of two-factor interactions. An example of a side-by-side plot is presented in Figure 4.1, which graphs the cell means for the social facilitation study. This strategy involves presenting separate two-factor graphs for each level of the second-order moderator variable. For population data, if there is no three-way interaction, then the patterning of the lines in each graph should be the same. In Figure 4.1, the patterning is different, with a steeper and more divergent line for complex tasks relative to simple tasks in the important conditions as opposed to the unimportant conditions.

5. ADDITIONAL CONSIDERATIONS

The previous chapters presented basic issues for the analysis of interaction effects in fixed-effects, equal n factorial analysis of variance (ANOVA). This chapter briefly considers additional issues that often need to be taken into account.

5.1   Violation of Model Assumptions

The statistical model underlying Equation 1.2 makes a number of simplifying assumptions so that the sample statistics (i.e., the t or F ratios) have a sampling distribution that closely approximates the theoretical t or F distribution. In the case of the fixed-effects, between-subjects ANOVA, three crucial assumptions are that (a) the observations within a cell are randomly sampled, (b) the within-cell population variances are equal (also called the homogeneity of variance assumption), and (c) the within-cell population scores are independently and normally distributed. Our interest here is with the latter two assumptions.

The assumption of homogeneous variances frequently is violated in practice. A central question is how robust the F test is to violations of this assumption. It is impossible to summarize research on this issue succinctly because of the many different contrasts that are possible. Box (1954) shows that the F test is robust in terms of Type I errors if there are an equal number of observations in each group, if the scores in the populations are normally distributed, and if the ratio of the largest population variance to the smallest population variance does not exceed 3. This also tends to be true for unequal group sample sizes so long as the sample sizes are fairly close to one another and greater than 20. Heterogeneity of variance tends to be more problematic as the number of levels of the factors increases (Wilcox, Charlin, & Thompson, 1986), as sample sizes become smaller, and as group sample sizes become more divergent. In the case of unequal sample sizes, the effect on Type I error rates depends, in part, on whether the larger variances occur in groups with the smaller sample sizes or vice versa. When smaller sample sizes are selected from populations with smaller variances, the F test becomes conservative, yielding an actual Type I error rate less than the stated α. When smaller sample sizes are selected from populations with larger variances, the Type I error rate tends to exceed α. Milligan, Wong, and Thompson (1977) and Harwell, Rubinstein, and Hayes (1992) describe numerous scenarios of robustness and nonrobustness with respect to the homogeneity of variance assumption.

A common strategy to evaluate the potential problem of variance heterogeneity is to apply a formal statistical test for variance heterogeneity and then proceed with standard ANOVA if the null hypothesis of equal variances is not rejected. Among the tests commonly used are those by Brown and Forsythe (1974) (i.e., Brown-Forsythe), Cochran (1941), Hartly (1950), and Scheffé (1959) (i.e., Box-Scheffé). However, these tests are problematic because many of them are sensitive to non-normality, they often lack statistical power, and they often fail to adequately control Type I errors when used as a "screen" for traditional ANOVA (e.g., Conover, Johnson, & Johnson, 1981; Games, Winkler, & Probert, 1972; Wilcox, 1992a). In light of this, several methodologists suggest using simple rules of thumb such as the following: *If the largest sample variance estimate is more than two or three times larger than the smallest sample variance, then consider alternative analytic strategies.* We know little about the utility of such heuristics at this point.

One strategy for dealing with variance heterogeneity is to perform analyses to identify outliers that may be causing the heterogeneity. Outliers are small numbers of observations that are highly discrepant from the general pattern of data and that mask fundamental trends within it. It may be that the source of the variance heterogeneity is due to such outliers. Once identified, the outliers can be eliminated from the analysis. If outliers are dropped, then it is essential that the researcher identify defining characteristics of the outlier cases so that generalizations can be tempered accordingly. For example, a study of sexual behavior in college students might find that outliers are older married students who are returning to college after many years away from school. Such students might be dropped from the analysis and conclusions applied to a population that explicitly excludes such students. Alternative methods for dealing with outliers are discussed by Hoaglin, Mosteller, and Tukey (1983). For a discussion of methods for identifying outliers, see Barnett and Lewis (1984).

A second strategy for dealing with variance heterogeneity is to transform the dependent variable so as to make the variances more homogeneous. This makes sense when the metric of the dependent variable is arbitrary, as described in Chapter 2. Transformation strategies are discussed in Hoaglin et al. (1983) and Rasmussen (1989). Budescu and Applebaum (1981) discuss difficulties with using variance-stabilizing transformations and report cases in which such transformations create problems rather than alleviate them.

A third approach for dealing with variance heterogeneity is to use a parametric alternative to ANOVA that does not rely on pooled error terms. A popular approach is an approximate degrees of freedom (ADF) solution based on the work of Welch (1951). The approach, as applied to single degree of freedom contrasts in fixed-effects, between-subjects ANOVA uses the following equation (Kirk, 1995; see also Olejnik, 1984) defined here for the case of four means so as to parallel Equation 1.2:

$$t = \frac{c_1 \overline{X}_{11} + c_2 \overline{X}_{12} + c_3 \overline{X}_{21} + c_4 \overline{X}_{22}}{\sqrt{(s_{11}^2 \frac{c_1^2}{n_{11}}) + (s_{12}^2 \frac{c_2^2}{n_{12}}) + (s_{21}^2 \frac{c_3^2}{n_{21}}) + (s_{22}^2 \frac{c_4^2}{n_{22}})}} \tag{5.1}$$

where s_{ij}^2 is the variance estimate for the cell characterized by Level i of Factor A and Level j of Factor B. The t value is compared against a critical t that has degrees of freedom equal to

$$df = \frac{(\sum_{j=1}^{k} c_j^2 s_j^2 / n_j)^2}{\sum_{j=1}^{k} [(c_j^2 s_j^2 / n_j)^2 / (n_j - 1)]}$$

where k is the total number of groups (in a 2 x 2 design, k = 4), and the single subscripts refer to the respective group means and variances, but notated here with a single subscript for simplification (i.e., group 2, group 3, and group 4).

Note that Equation 5.1 does not use the error term from the ANOVA summary table (i.e., MS_{ERROR}); instead, it forms a weighted combination of the separate group variances. Aside from this, the basic logic of the Welch method is comparable to our previous discussions using Equation 1.2.[14]

Lix and Keselman (1995) extend the logic of the Welch method to complex between-subjects and within-subjects factorial designs as well as to multiple comparison procedures that control experimentwise error rates. An alternative ADF approach is the James (1951) second-order method, which generally performs better than the Welch approach but is more difficult to implement. Wilcox (1989) presents a simplified variant of the

James second-order method. Although ADF approaches are reasonable in a wide array of research contexts, studies have found their performance to be suboptimal in conditions involving highly skewed populations (e.g., Wilcox, 1990). A promising approach for designs with more than two levels per factor that seems to work in some non-normal situations is presented by Alexander and Govern (1994).

A fourth approach to dealing with heterogeneous variances is to use a nonparametric method of analysis. One of the more commonly used methods is based on rank transformations (Conover & Iman, 1982). Rank transformation methods shift the conceptual question of interest because they do not necessarily represent tests of population means. Fligner and Policello (1982) describe a method for comparing group medians that uses a formulation similar to that of the Welch procedure but applied to ranks (see also Mee, 1990). More general discussions of rank transformation procedures can be found in Akritas (1991), Conover and Iman (1982), and Thompson (1991).

A final approach for confronting heterogeneous variances is to use statistical methods based on robust estimators such as trimmed means. Wilcox (1995) provides a useful and readable summary of robust estimators in this regard.

In designs involving within-subjects variables, the counterpart to the homogeneity of variance assumption is the assumption of sphericity (see Kirk, 1995, for a detailed discussion of the concept of sphericity). Classic tests for sphericity violations (e.g., Mauchly's test) have proven to be problematic due to low statistical power and sensitivity to non-normality. Cornell, Young, Seaman, and Kirk (1992) evaluate eight tests of sphericity and find that the locally best invariant test (Nago, 1973) has many desirable properties. Kirk (1995) recommends that the test be used to determine the appropriateness of the traditional repeated-measures ANOVA, but using an alpha level of .25 when the sample size is small and .15 when the sample size is larger than 10. Given violations of sphericity, Quintana and Maxwell (1994) suggest a modified degree of freedom test based on a combined Geisser-Greenhouse and Huyhn-Feldt weighting factor. Maxwell and Delaney (1990) discuss procedures for decomposing interactions under conditions of sphericity violation that do not rely on pooled error terms. Lix and Keselman (1995) and Keselman (1994) discuss robust multiple comparison procedures in these scenarios.

In terms of the assumption of normality, studies have suggested that the traditional F test in ANOVA is quite robust, especially when sample sizes are equal (or near equal) and greater than 15. Kurtosis tends to have little effect on Type I errors but can have effects on Type II errors when sample sizes are small (Kirk, 1995). The robustness of the test also is evident if the populations defined by the groups are homogeneous in form (e.g., all show about the same degrees of skewness and kurtosis). When this is not the case, the F test can be problematic (e.g., Cressie & Whitford, 1986). Preliminary tests of non-normality are not satisfactory because of their low statistical power. Remedial steps for non-normality can be taken in terms of outlier detection, transformations, use of nonparametric methods, or use of robust estimators, as discussed earlier (see Kirk, 1995, and Wilcox, 1995).

5.2 Unequal Sample Sizes

When sample sizes are unequal in factorial designs, some of the independent variables in the design may be confounded. This means that a portion of the variance in the dependent variable that is explained by one factor also may be explained by another factor. The traditional approach to dealing with this problem is to evaluate the significance of an effect in terms of its unique explained variance, eliminating from consideration any explained variance it has in common with other factors. An excellent discussion of the issues involved is provided by Maxwell and Delaney (1990). Computational methods for accommodating unequal sample sizes can be complex and are best executed with computers. For a discussion of computational methods, see Kirk (1995).

With unequal sample sizes in the two-factor design, the main effects typically will exhibit some degree of confounding; hence, their tests of significance will be affected accordingly. However, the test of the interaction effect is not affected. For three-factor and higher order designs, tests of interaction are affected if the interactions average over another factor. For example, in a three-factor design with unequal sample sizes, all of the two-way interactions typically will be confounded because each of them is averaged across a third factor. However, the three-way interaction is not confounded. When conducting contrasts on factors that are confounded with other factors, many researchers conduct the contrasts on means after they have been adjusted to remove the confounded explained variance of the other factors. This is readily accomplished with the aid of computers, as discussed shortly.

5.3   Measurement Error

The validity of inferences about group differences in population means with respect to some construct is influenced by the quality of the measures used to reflect that construct. We briefly consider the effects of two types of measurement error. The first type of error focuses on scale metric, where, for example, we assume that our data are interval level when, in fact, they are ordinal level. Of interest is whether such an error affects our ability to make accurate inferences with respect to group differences on the population mean of the underlying construct. A large number of measures in the social sciences are ordinal in character. However, these data still can be effectively analyzed using statistics that assume interval-level measures if departures from equal interval properties are not extreme. This latter statement requires elaboration.

Some researchers erroneously refer to scales as being interval or ordinal in character. It is important to recognize that metric qualities are not inherent in scales; rather, they are inherent in data and, hence, are influenced by all of the facets of data collection. The extent to which a set of measures has interval properties is dependent not only on the scale used to make observations but also on the particular set of individuals on which the observations are made, the time at which the data are collected, the setting in which the data are collected, and so on. Consider the following simplistic yet pedagogically useful example. The heights of five individuals are measured on two different metrics, inches and a rank order of height:

Individual	Height in Inches	Rank-Order Height
A	72	5
B	71	4
C	70	3
D	69	2
E	67	1

As is well known, the measures taken in inches have interval-level properties. For example, a difference of 1 between any two scores corresponds to the same physical difference on the underlying dimension of height. The actual height difference between Individuals A and B corresponds to the same true underlying height difference between Individuals C and D, and the metric reflects this (i.e., $72 - 71 = 1$ and $70 - 69 = 1$). Similarly, the difference between Individuals D and E is $69 - 67 = 2$, and the difference between Individuals A and C is 2. These differences also reflect the same amount on the underlying dimension of height. Note, however, that these properties do not hold for the rank-order measures. The difference in scores between Individuals A and B is 1 (i.e., $5 - 4$), and the difference in scores for Individuals D and E also is 1 (i.e., $2 - 1$). These identical differences correspond to differing degrees of height disparities (i.e., the true difference between Individuals D and E is larger than the true difference between Individuals A and B, as is evident for the measure using inches). For these individuals, the rank-order measures have ordinal properties but not interval properties.

Now consider five different individuals with the following scores:

Individual	Height in Inches	Rank-Order Height
A	72	5
B	71	4
C	70	3
D	69	2
E	68	1

Note that for these five individuals, the rank-order measures have interval-level properties. The difference in scores between Individuals A and B is 1, as is the difference in scores between Individuals D and E. These differences correspond to the exact same distance on the underlying physical dimension. In this case, what we think of as traditionally being an ordinal "scale" actually yields measures with interval-level properties. Suppose that Individual E was not 68 inches tall but instead was 67.9 inches tall. In this case, the rank-order measures are not strictly interval. However, they are close and probably can be treated as if they are interval level.

This example illustrates that the crucial analytic issue is not whether a set of measures is interval or ordinal. Rather, the critical issue is the extent to which a set of measures *approximates* interval-level characteristics. If the approximation is close, then the data often can be effectively analyzed using statistical methods that assume interval-level properties. If the approximation is poor, then an alternative analytic strategy is needed. In terms of tests of mean equality, Davison and Sharma (1988) show that the ANOVA of severely noninterval data still will be sensitive to mean differences on the underlying construct. However, it may be the case that nonparametric alternatives have greater statistical power and that these alternatives should be pursued instead. For a discussion of such alternatives, see Wilcox (1992b, 1996) and Cliff (1996). Departures from equal interval properties also adversely affect the estimation of confidence intervals and effect sizes. Hedges and Olkin (1984) describe several nonparametric estimators of effect size based on the logic of δ that may be useful in these contexts, and Wilcox (1996) and Jaccard and Becker (1996) describe nonparametric effect size indexes based on measures of association.

In terms of interaction effects, the issue of ordinal versus interval measurement is critical because departures from equal interval properties may produce statistically significant interactions when none is present. This issue is discussed by Anderson (1982) and Busemeyer and Jones (1983). When one suspects that an interaction is a measurement artifact, one can pursue transformations to eliminate the interaction (see Anderson, 1982; Kruskal, 1965; Winer, Brown, & Michaels, 1991).

Another facet of measurement that is relevant to the analysis of means is the unreliability of the dependent measure. In general, the more unreliable the dependent measure, the lower the statistical power of the analysis (Kopriva & Shaw, 1991). With unreliable measures, the parameter estimate in the numerator of Equation 1.2 will be unbiased given that there are no covariates in the design. However, the estimate of the standard error will be biased, as will the confidence intervals, in the direction of yielding too wide an interval. Unreliable measures produce bias in standardized indexes of effect size (e.g., d, partial epsilon squared) as well as in their estimated standard errors and confidence intervals. Hunter and Schmidt (1994) discuss methods for correcting measures of effect size for attenuation due to unreliability. Unreliable measures can, in some circumstances, create false interaction effects if the degree of unreliability differs in groups defined by the factorial design and the design includes covariates. Within the context of ANOVA paradigms, structural equation models with multiple indicators can be used to compare group means, taking into account complex error theories among the measures (e.g., Jöreskog & Sörbom, 1993). However, these methods require a large N.

5.4 Computer Analysis

All of the major statistical packages offer programs that permit the application of the methods described in this monograph. Most packages include options for "contrast analyses" or for defining parameter estimates within their ANOVA subroutines. STATISTICA for Windows offers "point-

and-click" applications of contrast codes to factorial designs, where all of the cell means are laid out as a single row vector, just as we have done in this monograph. SPSS for Windows permits users to specify contrasts and also provides detailed information on parameter estimates within the multiple ANOVA and general linear model subroutines. This also is true of the general linear model program for SAS. Care must be taken when interpreting the parameter estimates and contrast results yielded by these packages because the nature of the default contrasts and parameter estimates that are reported are different from one package to the next. In addition, the packages differ in whether the reported contrasts and parameter estimates adjust for unequal sample sizes and covariates. It is becoming increasingly necessary to have a basic understanding of the general linear model, dummy variable coding, and the nature of product terms in the linear model to gain an understanding of the output of contrasts and parameter estimates in statistical packages. The appendix offers guidelines in this regard. A document on how to apply the GLM procedure in SPSS to contrast analysis for unequal n, repeated measure designs, and covariates is available from the author upon request.

5.5 Concluding Comments

The method for analyzing interaction effects in factorial ANOVA is a complex topic on which reasonable statisticians can disagree. We have raised a number of issues and have proposed methods and perspectives for dealing with those issues in applied data-analytic settings. We recognize that our approach has limitations, that it will not be applicable in all contexts, and that researchers may prefer alternative approaches in the context of a given data-analytic situation. Nevertheless, we believe that the issues we have raised are important and that the method we suggest will be useful in a large number of analytic contexts.

APPENDIX:
Parameter Estimates
in the General Linear Model

This appendix describes the interpretation of regression coefficients in the general linear model with dummy variables and product terms. Knowledge of these rules will assist in the interpretation of parameter estimates typically reported by computer packages in the context of analysis of variance (ANOVA) programs or general linear model programs. We initially use the 3×2 example on desired family size from Chapter 4 and sample notation. We assume familiarity with the basics of multiple regression.

The general linear model can be stated as a multiple regression equation such that

$$Y = a + b_1 X_1 + b_2 X_2 + \ldots + b_k X_k + e.$$

Qualitative variables or factors from an experiment can be included in the model by using dummy variables. A dummy variable is a variable that is created by the analyst to represent group membership on a factor. For example, we can create a dummy variable and assign a value of 1 to all religious individuals and a value of 0 to all nonreligious individuals so as to represent religiosity, D_R. When a qualitative variable has more than two levels, it is necessary to specify more than one dummy variable to capture membership in the different groups. In general, one will need $k - 1$ dummy variables, where k is the number of levels of the factor. In the case of religion, we need $3 - 1 = 2$ dummy variables. For the first dummy variable, D_C, we assign all Catholics a value of 1 and everyone else a value of 0. For the second dummy variable, D_P, we assign all Protestants a value of 1 and everyone else a value of 0. Although we could create a third dummy variable for Jews, it is not necessary because it is redundant with the other two dummy variables. Once we know whether someone is Catholic and whether someone is Protestant (by means of the first two dummy variables), we know whether he or she is a Jew. The reasoning behind this might be more evident if one considers the religiosity dummy variable. We created a single dummy variable in which religious individuals were assigned a value of 1 and nonreligious individuals a value of 0. If we created a second dummy variable that assigned a value of 1 to nonreligious individuals and a value of 0 to religious individuals, then it would be perfectly negatively correlated with the first dummy variable and, hence, redundant.

There are different ways in which scores can be assigned to a dummy variable. We used a method called *dummy* scoring (or *simple* coding) that relies on 1's and 0's. *Effect* coding (also called *deviation* coding) uses 1's, 0's, and –1's, and orthogonal coding involves yet a different scoring scheme. Hardy (1993) discusses the logic of different coding schemes. We will develop rules for interpreting parameter estimates for the case of dummy coding. With dummy coding, the group that does not receive a 1 on any of the dummy variables for a given factor is called the *reference group* for that factor. For religiosity, the reference group is nonreligious individuals; for religion, the reference group is Jews. The choice of which group is the reference group is arbitrary from a statistical point of view.

Interaction effects are incorporated into the general linear model by using product terms, whereby we multiply all of the dummy variables for one factor by all of the dummy variables for another factor. In our example, we compute $D_R D_C$ and $D_R D_P$ to explore the interaction of religiosity and religion. We conduct a multiple regression with all of the dummy variables in the equation:

$$Y = a + b_1 D_R + b_2 D_C + b_3 D_P + b_4 D_R D_C + b_5 D_R D_P + e.$$

The unstandardized regression coefficients (b) reflect different parameter estimates. Each of the coefficients for the product terms refers to a single degree of freedom interaction contrast focused on a 2×2 subtable of the overall design. The subtable to which a given product term refers involves the groups scored 1 on the dummy variables within the product term and the reference groups for the two factors involved in the product term. For example, $D_R D_C$ refers to the 2×2 subtable for (Religious vs. Not Religious) $\times$ (Catholic vs. Jew). $D_R D_P$ refers to the 2×2 subtable for (Religious vs. Not Religious) $\times$ (Protestant vs. Jew). The value of the regression coefficient will equal the sample value of the interaction contrast in question. For example, the regression coefficient for $D_R D_C$ equals $(\overline{X}_{R,C} - \overline{X}_{NR,C}) - (\overline{X}_{R,J} - \overline{X}_{NR,J})$, where the subscript R stands for religious, NR stands for not religious, C stands for Catholic, P stands for Protestant, and J stands for Jew. In our sample data, $b_4 = 1.68$, which is interaction contrast IC_1 in Table 4.3. Using the same logic, b_5 reflects $(\overline{X}_{R,P} - \overline{X}_{NR,P}) - (\overline{X}_{R,J} - \overline{X}_{NR,J})$, which is IC_2 in Table 4.3. The tests of statistical significance of these regression coefficients will yield identical t values to those reported in Table 4.3.

The presence of the product terms in the equation alters the interpretation of the regression coefficients for the components of the various product terms (b_1 through b_3) relative to when the product terms are omitted. Consider b_1 for D_R. Without the product terms, b_1 would equal the main-effect mean difference between the group scored 1 on the dummy variable and the reference group, $(\overline{X}_R - \overline{X}_{NR})$. However, when the product terms that use D_R are included, b_1 becomes a conditional coefficient, namely the mean difference for the group scored 1 on D_R minus the group scored 0 on D_R, *conditioned on the other terms in the product term being equal to zero* (i.e., for $D_C = 0$ and $D_P = 0$). As it turns out, the Jews reference group defines the case in which $D_C = 0$ and $D_P = 0$. This means that b_1 equals the mean difference between religious individuals and nonreligious individuals when the focus is only on Jews (i.e., $\overline{X}_{R,J} - \overline{X}_{NR,J}$). b_1 is essentially a simple main effect for religiosity at the Jews level, and it equals SME_3 in Table 4.3.

Using this same logic, if the product terms were omitted, then b_2 would equal the mean difference between the group scored 1 on that dummy variable and the reference group for that factor $(\overline{X}_C - \overline{X}_J)$. When the product terms are included, b_2 reflects the difference in means between Catholics and Jews, conditioned on the other terms in the product term being equal to zero (i.e., for $D_R = 0$). b_2 represents the simple main effect for Catholics versus Jews for nonreligious individuals, a simple main effect in which we were not interested theoretically and which we did not compute. Finally, b_3 is the simple main effect for Protestants versus Jews for nonreligious individuals, again a simple main effect that was not of theoretical interest. In general, all of the coefficients in the equation are adjusted for unequal sample sizes (in the sense described in Chapter 5) and for any covariates that may be included in the equation.

When parameter estimates are requested from ANOVA computer programs that use the general linear model, the programs typically report the various b coefficients, and these are interpreted as we have just described (if the users have specified *dummy* coding or *simple* coding for the dummy variables). Note that each of these coefficients corresponds to a type of single degree of freedom contrast that we have discussed in this monograph. It is possible to isolate any single degree of freedom contrast by judicial choice of what the reference group is within a given computer run.

For the social facilitation example involving three factors, the relevant regression equation is

$$Y = a + b_1 D_{OP} + b_2 D_C + b_3 D_I + b_4 D_{OP} D_C + b_5 D_{OP} D_I + b_6 D_C D_I + b_7 D_{OP} D_C D_I + e,$$

where D_{OP} is a dummy variable for observer present (scored 1) versus absent (scored 0), D_C is a dummy variable for task complexity for which 1 = complex and 0 = simple, and D_I is a dummy variable for task importance for which 1 = important and 0 = not important. b_7 is the sample parameter value for the three-way interaction. For the facilitation study, it will equal –16.75 (see three-way interaction [TW] column in Table 4.6). b_4 refers to the parameter estimate for a 2 × 2 subtable focused on observer present versus observer absent and on the complex versus simple task. However, because the product term also appears within the three-way product term, b_4 is conditioned on the other terms in the three-way term being zero (i.e., $D_I = 0$). Thus, b_4 is a simple interaction contrast for the Observer × Task Complexity interaction when task importance is low (see SIE_1 in Table 4.6). Similar logic applies to b_5 and b_6.

Without the product terms, b_1 would reflect the difference between the main-effect means for observer present versus observer absent. However, because D_{OP} appears in other product terms involving D_C and D_I, it is conditioned on both D_C and D_I being 0. Thus, b_1 reflects a simple-simple main effect for the effect of observer when task complexity is simple and task importance is low (see $SSME_1$ in Table 4.6).

The key to interpreting (unstandardized) regression coefficients in the linear model with dummy variables and product terms is to keep in mind that (a) the coefficients associated with a given term always reflect a single degree of freedom contrast of the type discussed in this book and that (b) the coefficients for variables involved in higher order product terms are conditioned on other variables being equal to zero. Again, these statements hold true only for the case of dummy coding. For the interpretation of parameters for other forms of coding, see Kirk (1995).

Knowledge of the nature of parameter estimates in the general linear model is important to apply general linear model computer programs to accommodate unequal sample sizes and covariates. The formulas for executing contrasts in this book are straightforward when applied to the equal sample size case, but one typically must use computer programs when designs are unbalanced or include covariates.

NOTES

1. We focus our discussion on the case of factorial designs with equal cell sample sizes, and all of the statements we make in Chapters 1 to 4 assume this to be the case. We address the case of unequal cell sample sizes in Chapter 5.

2. The power analysis programs also can be used to determine the sample sizes necessary to achieve a given level of power for purposes of planning a study.

3. In the case of designs with within-subject factors, the use of MS_{ERROR} means that d is defined partialling out other factors in the design as well as across individual variation in the dependent variable. This may or may not be appropriate, depending on the theoretical questions being addressed.

4. The sum of squares for an effect corresponding to a main effect or interaction is obtained from the summary table of the ANOVA. A general formula for calculating SS_{EFFECT} for any contrast that uses Equation 1.2 in the equal n case is $SS_{EFFECT} = (\Sigma c_j T_j)^2 / (n \Sigma c_j^2)$, where T is the sum of scores in Condition j, c is the contrast coefficient associated with Condition j, and the summation is across all conditions in the numerator of Equation 1.2.

5. Omega squared, however, is not an unbiased estimator; rather, it tends to show a small degree of negative bias.

6. These criticisms concerning metric and the arbitrariness of magnitude of the manipulation apply with equal force to classic hypothesis testing and F tests in the context of ANOVA.

7. Cohen does not discuss the criteria for declaring an effect size to be trivial and, hence, ignorable.

8. We use the term *reasonably confident* in the sense implied by the theory underlying confidence intervals: If one were to select an infinite number of samples and calculate confidence intervals in each sample using the procedures described, then the true value of the population parameter would be contained in those intervals in 95% of the cases.

9. This analysis normally should be conducted before the study is implemented to ensure that statistical power is adequate.

10. When differences in conclusions based on the interval estimation approach occur as a function of the index examined (e.g., means of raw scores vs. partial epsilon squared), we recommend that priority be given to the results from the analysis of raw means. The statistical theory and robustness of this approach is much further developed than that for the other indexes. In our opinion, it usually is more prudent to work with units of raw means, and this would require researchers focused on standardized TVs (based on δ or percentage of explained variance) to convert them to raw score units.

11. As noted earlier, it is possible to use classic null hypothesis testing with non-zero TVs.

12. The Scheffé critical value also can be used to form simultaneous confidence intervals.

13. The Tukey-based critical value also can be used to form simultaneous confidence intervals.

14. As Maxwell and Delaney (1990) point out, the MS_{ERROR} in the classic ANOVA also is a combination of the separate group variance, but a different weighting and combinatorial scheme is used.

REFERENCES

ABELSON, R. P. (1985) "A variance explanation paradox: When a little is a lot." *Psychological Bulletin, 97,* 129-133.

ABELSON, R. P. (1995) *Statistics as Principled Argument.* Hillsdale, NJ: Lawrence Erlbaum.

AKRITAS, M.G. (1991) "Limitations of the rank transform procedure: A study of repeated measures designs, part I." *Journal of the American Statistical Association, 86,* 457-460.

ALEXANDER, R. A., & GOVERN, D. M. (1994) "A new and simpler approximation for ANOVA under variance heterogeneity." *Journal of Educational Statistics, 19,* 91-101.

ALGINA, J., & OLEJNIK, S. F. (1984) "Implementing the Welch-James procedure with factorial designs." *Educational and Psychological Measurement, 44,* 39-48.

ANDERSON, N. H. (1982) *Methods of Information Integration.* New York: Academic Press.

BARNETT, V., & LEWIS, T. (1984) *Outliers in Statistical Data.* New York: John Wiley.

BERNHARDSON, C. S. (1975) "Type I error rates when multiple comparison procedures follow a significant F test of ANOVA." *Biometrics, 31,* 229-232.

BOIK, R. J. (1993) "The analysis of two-factor interactions in fixed effects linear models." *Journal of Educational Statistics, 18,* 1-40.

BOX, G. E. P. (1954) "Some theorems on quadratic forms applied in the study of analysis of variance problems: I. Effects of inequality of variance in the one way model." *Annals of Statistics, 25,* 290-302.

BROWN, M. B., & FORSYTHE, A. B. (1974) "Robust tests for the equality of variances." *Journal of the American Statistical Association, 69,* 364-367.

BUDESCU, D. V., & APPLEBAUM, M. I. (1981) "Variance stabilizing transformations and the power of the F test." *Journal of Educational Statistics, 6,* 55-74.

BUSEMEYER, J., & JONES, L. (1983) "Analysis of multiplicative combination rules when the causal variables are measured with error." *Psychological Bulletin, 93,* 549-562.

CHOW, S. L. (1988) "Significance test or effect size?" *Psychological Bulletin, 103,* 105-110.

CHOW, S. L. (1989) "Significance tests and deduction: Reply to Folger (1989)." *Psychological Bulletin, 106,* 161-165.

CICCHETTI, D. V. (1972) "Extension of multiple range tests to interaction tables in the analysis of variance: A rapid approximation solution." *Psychological Bulletin, 77,* 405-408.

CLIFF, N. (1996) *Ordinal Methods for Behavioral Data Analysis.* Mahwah, NJ: Lawrence Erlbaum.

COCHRAN, W. G. (1941) "The distribution of the largest of a set of estimated variances as a fraction of their total." *Annals of Eugenics, 11,* 47-52.

COHEN, J. (1988) *Statistical Power Analysis for the Behavioral Sciences.* Hillsdale, NJ: Lawrence Erlbaum.

COHEN, J. (1994) "The earth is round ($p < .05$)." *American Psychologist, 49,* 997-1003.

CONOVER, W. J., & IMAN, R. L. (1981) "Rank transformations as a bridge between parametric and non-parametric statistics." *American Statistician, 35,* 124-129.

CONOVER, W. J., JOHNSON, M. E., & JOHNSON, M. M. (1981) "A comparative study of tests of homogeneity of variances with applications to the outer continental shelf bidding data." *Technometrics, 23,* 351-361.

CORNELL, J. E., YOUNG, D. M., SEAMAN, S. L., & KIRK, R. E. (1992) "Power comparisons of eight tests for sphericity in repeated measures designs." *Journal of Educational Statistics, 17,* 233-249.

CORTINA, J. M., & DUNLAP, W. P. (1997) "On the logic and purpose of significance testing." *Psychological Methods, 2,* 161-172.

CRESSIE, N. A., & WHITFORD, H. J. (1986) "How to use the two sample *t* test." *Biometrical Journal, 28,* 131-148.

DAVISON, M., & SHARMA, A. (1988) "Parametric statistics and levels of measurement." *Psychological Bulletin, 104,* 137-144.

DUNCAN, D. B. (1955) "Multiple range and multiple *F* tests." *Biometrics, 11,* 1-42.

FEINGOLD, A. (1995) "The additive effects of differences in central tendency and variability are important in comparisons between groups." *American Psychologist, 50,* 5-13.

FLEISS, J. L. (1986) "Significance tests have a role in epidemiologic research: Reactions to A. M. Walker." *American Journal of Public Health, 76,* 559-560.

FLIGNER, M. A., & POLICELLO, G. E. (1982) "Robust rank procedures for the Behrens-Fisher problem." *Journal of the American Statistical Association, 76,* 162-168.

FOLGER, R. (1989) "Significance tests and the duplicity of binary decisions." *Psychological Bulletin, 106,* 155-160.

FOWLER, R. L. (1984) "Approximating probability levels for testing null hypotheses with noncentral *F* distributions." *Educational and Psychological Measurement, 44,* 275-281.

FOWLER, R. L. (1985) "Point estimates and confidence intervals in measures of association." *Psychological Bulletin, 98,* 160-165.

FOWLER, R. L. (1986) "Confidence intervals for the cross validated multiple correlation in predictive regression models." *Journal of Applied Psychology, 71,* 318-322.

FOWLER, R. L. (1988) "Estimating the standardized mean difference in intervention studies." *Journal of Educational Statistics, 13,* 337-350.

GABRIEL, K. R., PUTTER, J., & WAX, Y. (1973) "Simultaneous confidence intervals for product-type interaction contrasts." *Journal of Royal Statistical Society, 35,* 234-244.

GAMES, P. A., WINKLER, H., & PROBERT, D. A. (1972) "Robust tests for homogeneity of variance." *Educational and Psychological Measurement, 32,* 887-909.

GASTORF, J. W. (1980) "Time urgency and the Type A behavior pattern." *Journal of Consulting and Clinical Psychology, 48,* 299.

GIGERENZER, G. (1993) "The superego, the ego, and the id in statistical reasoning." In G. Keren & C. Lewis (Eds.). *A Handbook for Data Analysis in the Behavioral Sciences: Methodological Issues* (pp. 311-339). Hillsdale, NJ: Lawrence Erlbaum.

HARDY, K. (1993) *Regression With Dummy Variables.* Newbury Park, CA: Sage.

HARTLEY, H. O. (1950) "The maximum F ratio as a short cut test for heterogeneity of variance." *Biometrika, 37,* 308-312.

HARWELL, M. R., RUBINSTEIN, E. N., & HAYES, W. (1992) "Summarizing Monte Carlo results in methodological research: The one and two factor fixed effects ANOVA cases." *Journal of Educational Statistics, 17,* 315-339.

HEDGES, L. V., & OLKIN, I. (1984) "Nonparametric estimators of effect size in meta-analysis." *Psychological Bulletin, 96,* 573-580.

HOAGLIN, D. C., MOSTELLER, F., & TUKEY, J. W. (1983) *Understanding Robust and Exploratory Data Analysis.* New York: John Wiley.

HOCHBERG, Y. (1988) "A sharper Bonferroni procedure for multiple tests of significance." *Biometrika, 75,* 800-802.

HOLLAND, B. S., & COPENHAVER, M. (1988) "Improved Bonferroni-type multiple testing procedures." *Psychological Bulletin, 104,* 145-149.

HOLM, S. (1979) "A simple sequentially rejective multiple test procedure." *Scandinavian Journal of Statistics, 6,* 65-70.

HOWSON, C., & URBACH, P. (1989) *Scientific Reasoning: The Bayesian Approach.* La Salle, IL: Open Court.

HUNTER, J. E., & SCHMIDT, F. L. (1994) "Correcting for sources of artificial variation across studies." In H. Cooper & L. Hedges (Eds.), *The Handbook of Research Synthesis.* New York: Russell Sage.

JACCARD, J., & BECKER, M. (1996) *Statistics for the Behavioral Sciences.* Pacific Grove, CA: Brooks/Cole.

JAMES, G. S. (1951) "The comparison of several groups of observations when the ratios of the population variances are unknown." *Biometrika, 38,* 324-329.

JÖRESKOG, K., & SÖRBOM, D. (1993) *LISREL VIII.* Chicago: Scientific Software.

KEPPEL, G. (1991) *Design and Analysis: A Researcher's Handbook.* Englewood Cliffs, NJ: Prentice Hall.

KESELMAN, H. J. (1994) "Stepwise and simultaneous multiple comparison procedures for repeated measures' means." *Journal of Educational Statistics, 19,* 127-162.

KIRK, R. (1995) *Experimental Design: Procedures for the Behavioral Sciences.* Pacific Grove, CA: Brooks/Cole.

KOPRIVA, R. J., & SHAW, D. G. (1991) "Power estimates: The effect of dependent variable reliability on the power of one factor ANOVAs." *Educational and Psychological Measurement, 51,* 585-595.

KROMERY, J. D., & DICKINSON, W. B. (1995) "The use of an overall F test to control Type I error rates in factorial analysis of variance: Limitations and better strategies." *Journal of Applied Behavioral Science, 31,* 51-64.

KRUSKAL, J. B. (1965) "Analysis of factorial experiments by estimating monotone transformations of the data." *Journal of the Royal Statistical Society, 27,* 251-263.

LIX, L. M., & KESELMAN, H. J. (1995) "Approximate degrees of freedom tests: A unified perspective on testing for mean equality." *Psychological Bulletin, 117,* 547-560.

MARASCULIO, L. A., & LEVIN, J. R. (1970) "Appropriate post hoc comparisons for interaction and nested hypotheses in analysis of variance designs: The elimination of Type IV errors." *American Educational Research Journal, 7,* 397-421.

MAXWELL, S. E., CAMP, C. J., & ARVEY, R. D. (1981) "Measures of strength of association: A comparative examination." *Journal of Applied Psychology, 66,* 525-534.

MAXWELL, S. E., & DELANEY, H. D. (1990) *Designing Experiments and Analyzing Data: A Model Comparison Perspective.* Belmont, CA: Wadsworth.

McGRAW, K. O., & WONG, S. P. (1992) "A common language effect size statistic." *Psychological Bulletin, 111,* 361-365.

MEE, R. W. (1990) "Confidence intervals for probabilities and tolerance regions based on a generalization of the Mann-Whitney statistic." *Journal of the American Statistical Association, 85,* 793-800.

MEEHL, P. E. (1990a) "Appraising and amending theories: The strategy of Lakatosian defense and two principles that warrant it." *Psychological Inquiry, 1,* 108-141.

MEEHL, P. E. (1990b) "Why summaries of research on psychological theories are often uninterpretable." *Psychological Reports, 66,* 195-244.

MEYER, D. L. (1991) "Misinterpretation of interaction effects: A reply to Rosnow and Rosenthal." *Psychological Bulletin, 110,* 571-573.

MILLIGAN, G. W., WONG, D. S., & THOMPSON, P. A. (1987) "Robustness properties of nonorthogonal analysis of variance." *Psychological Bulletin, 101,* 464-470.

NAGO, H. (1973) "On some test criteria for covariance matrix." *Annals of Statistics, 1,* 700-709.

PETTY, R. E., FABRIGAR, L. R., WEGENER, D. T., & PRIESTER, J. R. (1996) "Understanding data when interactions are present or hypothesized." *Psychological Science, 7,* 247-252.

PHILLIPS, L. D. (1973) *Bayesian Statistics for Social Scientists.* London: Nelson.

POLLARD, W. (1985) *Bayesian Statistics for Evaluation Research: An Introduction.* Beverly Hills, CA: Sage.

PRENTICE, D. A., & MILLER, D. T. (1992) "When small effects are impressive." *Psychological Bulletin, 112,* 160-164.

QUINTANA, S. M., & MAXWELL, S. E. (1994) "A Monte Carlo comparison of seven ε adjustment procedures in repeated measures designs with small sample sizes." *Journal of Educational Statistics, 19,* 57-71.

RASMUSSEN, J. L. (1989) "Data transformations, Type I error rate and power." *British Journal of Mathematical and Statistical Psychology, 42,* 203-211.

ROSENTHAL, R. (1994) "Parametric measures of effect size." In H. Cooper & L. V. Hedges (Eds.), *The Handbook of Research Synthesis* (pp. 231-244). New York: Russell Sage.

ROSENTHAL, R. (1995) "Methodology." In A. Tesser (Ed.), *Advanced Social Psychology* (pp. 17-50). New York: McGraw-Hill.

ROSENTHAL, R., & ROSNOW, R. L. (1989) *Contrast Analysis: Focused Comparisons in the Analysis of Variance.* Cambridge, UK: Cambridge University Press.

ROSENTHAL, R., & RUBIN, D. B. (1994) "The counternull value of an effect size: A new statistic." *Psychological Science, 5,* 329-334.

ROSNOW, R. L., & ROSENTHAL, R. (1989a) "Definition and interpretation of interaction effects." *Psychological Bulletin, 105,* 143-146.

ROSNOW, R. L., & ROSENTHAL, R. (1989b) "Statistical procedures and the justification of knowledge in psychological science." *American Psychologist, 44,* 1276-1284.

ROSNOW, R. L., & ROSENTHAL, R. (1991) "If you're looking at the cell means, you're not looking *only* at the interaction (unless all main effects are zero)." *Psychological Bulletin, 110,* 574-576.

ROSNOW, R. L., & ROSENTHAL, R. (1996) "Contrasts and interaction effects redux: Five easy pieces." *Psychological Science, 7,* 253-257.

RYAN, T. A. (1962) "The experiment as the unit for computing rates of error." *Psychological Bulletin, 59,* 301-305.

SCHEFFÉ, H. (1959) *The Analysis of Variance.* New York: John Wiley.

SEAMAN, M. A., LEVIN, K. R., & SERLIN, R. C. (1991) "New developments in pairwise multiple comparisons: Some powerful and practicable procedures." *Psychological Bulletin, 110,* 577-586.

SHROUT, P. E. (1997) "Should significance tests be banned?" *Psychological Science, 8,* 1-2.

TANG, P. C. (1938) "The power function of the analysis of variance tests with tables and illustrations of their use." *Statistical Research Memoirs, 2,* 126-149.

THOMPSON, G. L. (1991) "A unified approach to rank tests for multivariate and repeated measures designs." *Journal of the American Statistical Association, 86,* 410-419.

TOOTHAKER, L. E. (1993) *Multiple Comparison Procedures.* Newbury Park, CA: Sage.

WELCH, B. L. (1951) "On the comparison of several mean values: An alternative approach." *Biometrika, 38,* 330-336.

WILCOX, R. R. (1989) "Adjusting for unequal variances when comparing means in one way and two way fixed effects ANOVA models." *Journal of Educational Statistics, 14,* 269-278.

WILCOX, R. R. (1990) "Comparing variances and means when distributions have non-identical shapes." *Communications in Statistics—Simulation and Computation, 19,* 155-173.

WILCOX, R. R. (1992a) "An improved method for comparing variances when distributions have non-identical shapes." *Computational Statistics and Data Analysis, 13,* 163-172.

WILCOX, R. R. (1992b) "Why can methods for comparing means have relatively low power, and what can you do to correct the problem?" *Current Directions in Psychological Science, 1,* 101-105.

WILCOX, R. R. (1995) "ANOVA: A paradigm for low power and misleading measure of effect size?" *Review of Educational Research, 65,* 51-77.

WILCOX, R. R. (1996) *Statistics for the Social Sciences.* New York: Academic Press.

WILCOX, R., CHARLIN, V., & THOMPSON, K. (1986) "New Monte Carlo results on the robustness of the ANOVA *F*, *W* and *F** statistics." *Communications in Statistics—Simulation and Computation, 15,* 933-943.

WILSON, W. (1962) "A note on the inconsistency inherent in the necessity to perform multiple comparisons." *Psychological Bulletin, 59,* 296-300.

WINER, B., BROWN, D. R., & MICHAELS, K. M. (1991) *Statistical Principles in Experimental Design.* New York: McGraw-Hill.

YEATON, W. H., & SECHREST, L. (1981) "Meaningful measures of effect." *Journal of Consulting and Clinical Psychology, 49,* 766-767.

ABOUT THE AUTHOR

JAMES JACCARD is Professor of Psychology at the University of Albany, State University of New York. He is director of the Center for Applied Psychological Research. His primary research interests are in the areas of the psychology of population dynamics and adolescent risk behavior, with an emphasis on adolescent unintended pregnancy and adolescent drunk driving. His work has focused on family-based approaches to dealing with adolescent problem behaviors.